BEFORE YOU START

GD DOWEY

The Beatitudes

ISBN 978-1-7359876-4-4
Library of Congress Control Number: 2023907154

Righteous Acts Publishing
Irmo, South Carolina

This little book is dedicated to my absolutely beautiful, loving, and amazing wife, Missie. I've never met anyone who embodies the Beatitudes like her.

Table of Contents

INTRODUCTION...I

ATTITUDE #1 • GET EMPTY 1

ATTITUDE #2 • START CRYING 13

ATTITUDE #3 • SEEK MEEK 27

ATTITUDE #4 • HUNGRY & THIRSTY 39

ATTITUDE #5 • MERCY LORD! 49

ATTITUDE #6 • PURITY.. 59

ATTITUDE #7 • ALL WE ARE SAYING............................ 71

ATTITUDE #8 • NEW RELIGION 83

ATTITUDE #9 • MOVING DAY 95

ACKNOWLEDGMENTS 107

ABOUT THE AUTHOR 109

OTHER BOOKS BY GD DOWEY 111

Introduction

Before you start jumping around and looking to do spiritual calisthenics in the Christian life make sure you have a firm footing in Christ. However, don't wait around, it's important to begin to grow in Jesus. The Sermon on the Mount is a fantastic planting field for your harvest that is to come from right living. So before you start complaining about not understanding the fresh life in Christ, **before you start** wandering away from your relationship with Christ, and **before you start** to end the sanctifying process of spiritual growth in Him, get rooted. It's the only way to grow!

I'm amazed more and more at the descriptions and pictures of following Christ that I draw from my grandfather. In the very late winter weeks, on the edge of the spring, my "Papa" would take his old frame and hook up the disc and plow attachment. He would then climb up on his 1951 Ford 8N tractor and begin to prepare the ground. The soil had become hard from the winter months and now needed to be plowed up to receive the seeds. Once the ground was softened, then you could lay out the rows and drop and cover the seed. Hosea says, *"Sow to yourselves in righteousness, reap in mercy; break up your fallow ground: for it is time to seek the Lord, till he come and rain righteousness upon you* (10:12 KJV)."

Before you start desiring to exercise some of your maturity in Christ, to serve, to give, to love, and continue to be faithful, you may need to allow the Word of God to soften your heart. It means to convict you of your attitude. That's what this book is about — your attitude. I like that old saying, *"People don't care about what you know, until they know that you care."* Having a spectacular attitude is tantamount to success for the Christ-follower. Many claim to be seeking after the Lord Jesus, but do we really care? All your acts of serving and giving don't amount to anything without the right righteous attitude.

When unwrapping new technology and getting started, there is often the caution in red, bold type: STOP! It's the warning in big letters, adjoined with an exclamation point to get you to pause and make sure you don't do anything to short-circuit or break your new toy, while following directions. I was infamous for discarding the instructions to put together my son's toys when he was a little boy. I can't count the times I had to go back and start over because I was too proud to follow simple directives. I scratch my head wondering how nuts I was not to read the guideline and commands for construction.

The Sermon on the Mount plows my hard heart and gives me directions on how to build a godly life. We just need to be reminded often to follow the instructions. Why don't Christian pulpiteers preach on the Beatitudes more often? Why isn't Matthew 5, 6, and 7 the center of our discipleship programs? What are we doing in studying on how to grow in Christ that is more important than grasping the vine and branch structure of Scripture that Jesus models in Matthew 5?

My prayer is that this little book helps you as you study to grow in your attitude toward the Spirit of God as He leads you. May you hook up the plow to disc your heart. May you sow with expectation, keeping the weeds from the plant. And may God begin to grow beautiful, healthy fruit in your life. **Before you start**, you must prepare the soil. **Before you start**, there is plowing of the soul to be done. **Before you start**, prepare your heart.

GD Dowey
Irmo, SC
June 2023

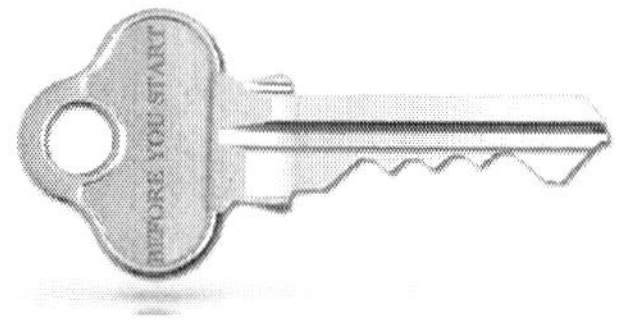

Attitude #1 • Get Empty

"Blessed are the poor in spirit, for theirs is the kingdom of heaven."
-Matthew 5:3

Every man must be settled without doubt that he was the man that crucified Christ.
-William Perkins

HOW do you live the studious, consistent, yet harmonious, God-fearing Christian life? It's difficult. Along with the means God has given us to live it — the Holy Spirit — there must be a starting point. So, where do you begin the Christ-following life? Make no mistake. Living for Jesus, by bowing to Him as your king, is your greatest assignment. But have you seen the size of the textbook? My college biology lab manual was easier to maneuver! The Bible is long, some parts of Scripture are laborious to get through. If we could just get a look at God, would that make His Word painless to study? I don't know of anything more difficult in my life than to give my life to this invisible God, yet I see Him all the time.

I struggle with my golf game. The consistency of my swing, my pace and tempo, cause me to bog down in the middle of play. My mechanics are all wrong. My approach is too frivolous. There are a million different golf teaching videos to purchase and download, a million instructors, and a gazillion friends who tell you just to have fun. Who do you listen to? Maybe I need a lesson. Or two. Or a hundred. Where do I go, who do I see? There are a myriad of options and schools of thought. Which one should I go with? Can't there be just one way? Do you struggle with the changing politics and the progression of our country? Everyone has an opinion or idea of how this country is to be governed. I was listening to our city's mayor during his inaugural speech this year and he actually said, "I am going to fix the problem of potholes in the roads of this city!" Part of me was, "All right! I hate those potholes!" And the other part of me was asking, "What?! You're elected to one of the highest offices in the city and potholes is our problem?" That's our problem? Potholes? Surely there's something else more pressing. Wasn't the issue of potholes also the problem fifty years ago?

Here's a golf-swing, pothole problem for us: we struggle with living the Christian life because it's bumpy and we are inconsistent. How do you do it right so that it's a little smoother? Seriously, how do you live life like Christ? That's our goal. Nothing enthuses me and fires me up like studying the saints of the past, many of them having been martyred for their faith in Christ. They sold out, gave out, and lived out everything in regard to Jesus. Does it seem to you that, while some of us battle with it, some people just have it all together in their relationship with Jesus? Is it even possible to do it like them?

I love the likes of spiritual giants of the past like Martin Luther, John Calvin, John Owen, Richard Sibbes, John Flavel, Charles Spurgeon, J. Gresham Machen, Martyn Lloyd-Jones; and missionaries like Hudson Taylor, Lottie Moon, and Adoniram Judson. Their courage in standing up to the status quo, and their actions standing on their faith in Christ, inspires me. I often look to their writings for wisdom and inspiration. However, they didn't all agree on every subject in the Bible. They had differences in their theologies and beliefs, so to pick one of them and copy their Christian lifestyle isn't feasible.

If you are like me, there have been times when I felt like I knew what God wanted, and then there were times I felt distant and lived in a foreign land. If you are asking me, and in a sense, you are — it's why you are reading this book — *How do I swing for accuracy and distance while riding on a bump-less road with God?* There is only One way, there is only One option, and there is only One teacher. There is only One to look to and only One sermon to study. This sermon, The Sermon on the Mount, was so good that whenever I preach and teach on it, my congregation knows that I refer to it simply as "The Sermon." In my opinion, you must grasp this sermon before you study any more in the Bible. It begins in a fairly discernible way. There is a crowd of people, and Jesus walks into the pulpit:

> *Seeing the crowds, he went up on the mountain, and when he sat down, his disciples came to him. And he opened his mouth and taught them, saying: "Blessed are the poor in spirit, for theirs is the kingdom of heaven."* -Matthew 5:1-3

Maybe you are already aware of the first few verses in Matthew 5, known as the Beatitudes. In verses 3-13, the Beatitudes are short sentences that Jesus begins with "*Blessed are....*" This is not the only spot in the Bible where beatitudes are discovered. It's a Latin word, *beati*, meaning *blessed.*

You find beatitudes in the Psalms. Psalm 1 says,

> *Blessed is the man who walks not in the counsel of the wicked, nor stands in the way of sinners, nor sits in the seat of scoffers; but his delight is in the law of the Lord, and on his law he meditates day and night.* -Psalm 1:1-2

What does blessing mean? Simply put, it's the opposite of curse. God says in the book of Deuteronomy that those who keep the covenant will be blessed and those who don't are cursed. Still, what does blessing mean? It's simply fellowship with God. God's covenant states that when we keep it, He says, "I will be your God and you will be My people." Sometimes you see it translated in modern Bible translations with the word, *happy*. It's fair language, but not as deep as the word *blessing*. Jesus is pointing out in the Psalms, and further in Isaiah, that we are to live blessed lives. Most Christ-followers have forgotten that — if they ever knew it in the first place. It's the normal Christian life. So, what is it?

The Beatitudes are meant to tell you and me how we get the answers to the questions in our lives. The Beatitudes tell us how to live a blessed life and not a cursed life. You desperately need to know the Beatitudes because they are EXACTLY how God intends for us to live. And we need to understand that they are in order. Here again, the first one:

> *"Blessed are the poor in spirit, for theirs is the kingdom of heaven."* —Matthew 5:3

There is no one in the Kingdom of God who is not poor in spirit. No one. It is the fundamental characteristic of the Christian and the citizen of heaven. No one can be a Christian without being poor in spirit. So, here's the question: how do I become a Christian and how do I live as a Christian? Here's the one word to take away with you as you read and study the first Beatitude:

EMPTY

Here's a hint about the upcoming Beatitudes — they all talk about being filled. Before you arrive at God's filling station, you must first start by getting empty. If there is any one-sentence, counter-cultural phrase in the entire New Testament, one that flies in the face of this world, it's this: *Blessed are the poor in spirit...for theirs is the Kingdom of heaven.* It goes against the grain. Maybe you cannot see it yet, but it's a slap in the face to Hollywood and Wall Street.

4

Just look at this statement and compare it to your life. Every morning we arise to go to work, and we look to fill our pockets with money. When we go to the grocery store, we want to fill our carts and baskets with food (good luck in today's economy). Going to school, we want to fill our minds. Fill, fill, fill is what we think about. Examine it and compare it and you will find that all of California, New York, the West coast, and the East coast despise being hungry. All of the District of Columbia, all of Paris, all of Shanghai, all of socialism, all of communism, the Democrats and the Republicans, and all of social media literally hate the word *empty*! It's the antithesis of everything every state University teaches. It's the opposite of every earthly doctrine and political party.

Everything you have ever learned is self-reliance, self-confidence, and self-expression. Ask any modern-day college professor or motivational guru and they will tell you that you must believe in yourself. That one idea controls the thought-life of this world. If you go for a job interview, you are reminded to put your best foot forward and make a lasting impression. Today's motto is the more successful we appear, the more successful we become. It's the whole idea of the American life and the American Dream. Express yourself, believe in yourself, realize your potential, visualize it, and become it! No one has ever walked into a job interview and said, "I am the worst of the worst. I am a sinner from the word go and I will steal, take advantage of you, and talk about you behind your back. I will organize against you and lead a revolt of this company! Hire me!"

Tell me one politician on the local level, the state level, or the national level that has been elected because of their humility. None. No one. Not a single one. Every politician I've ever heard of is elected because of their personality and fame or money. No political candidate comes to office as a quiet, honest, truthful, meek servant. Every politician says, "Vote for me because I will fill you up! I will give you what you want!" They paint that picture, but when Mr. and Mrs. Whomever goes to Washington, it turns out, they rarely deliver.

Even preachers and Christian teachers, today, are on ego kicks. Many are guilty of promoting themselves. Why? Fame, fortune, popularity, and being filled up! Rarely do you find a Christian minister or missionary being poor in spirit these days. The modern-day church and preacher overpromises and underdelivers. How often do you find Christians that are bankrupt in spirit? *But that's exactly where God wants you and me.* It's why I love to read missionary stories of those saints a hundred years ago. Most of them gave up their homes and families to follow Jesus to places you and I would defiantly refuse to visit. With those men and women who followed Christ before the modern age, you can point out the common denominator: they were being poor in spirit. If being poor in spirit is what really defines a true Christian, then how many true Christians do you really know?

What does it mean to be "poor in spirit?"

It doesn't mean to be nervous or afraid. It's not a weakness term. It has nothing to do with money. By the way, poverty and financial lack doesn't equate to a spiritual advantage to someone who is more affluent than you. Note this: no one is born "poor in spirit." A truly poor in spirit person doesn't worry about making a spiritual impression on others. Because if you are truly poor in spirit you will always make the right impression. Being poor in spirit is not false humility, it's not escaping this world, it's not changing your name, and it's not pretending. It's not being pretentious or false piety, nor is it playing like we are religious. Poor in spirit is not some religious gear we shift into on Sunday morning at 10 o'clock, only to shift back into "me" gear to live out the rest of the week.

I am aware that I have taken a prolonged, negative approach in defining being *poor in spirit.* My purpose is so that I can show you precisely what it means and how we are to apply it to our lives. The bottom line is we want to be where God is. If you desire the tranquil and peaceful life we are promised in Christ, then we must go to the prophet Isaiah. He writes,

It's an incredible verse! Where does God live? He lives with the poor in spirit. Everyone He works through in the Scriptures is *poor in spirit.* Everyone in this world, in whom God works for His purpose, is poor in spirit. We must not be fooled into thinking that if we are not poor in spirit, by denying our sinful cravings to be filled more, then there is another way. There isn't! I'm not talking about being filled with the Spirit here. Being filled with the Spirit is a whole different subject and book. Discovering the true meaning of being poor in spirit, humbling oneself before the Almighty and Sovereign, is essential to begin your spiritual growth and obedience to Him.

God told Gideon to rescue Israel from the armies of the enemy and look,

Gideon said to him, "Me, my master? How and with what could I ever save Israel? Look at me. My clan's the weakest in Manasseh and I'm the runt of the litter."

God said to him, "I'll be with you. Believe me, you'll defeat Midian as one man."
                                                         -Judges 6:15-16

Do you see Gideon's testimony of humility? To be poor in spirit is to be humble. To be poor in spirit is to completely rely upon Him. It is to seek to empty oneself of self, and to be filled with the Holy Spirit. When we realize He is truly with us, everything changes. The Apostle Paul said, "It's God with us, that is the hope of glory." The great reformer, Martin Luther, wrote,

I simply taught, preached, and wrote God's Word; otherwise, I did nothing. The Word did everything.

Moses was very conscious of his own insufficiency and inadequacy. When God called him to return to Egypt and lead His people out of captivity, Moses began making excuse after excuse. He told God he is a nobody, with no authority, and even told God that he has a stuttering problem. You just must love God's quick response and solution: *Tell them I'm with you.*

According to God, poor in spirit is learning and living a little more like this: It's not that you are too weak to do and live like God wants you to, but that you don't know how weak and incapable you are to live that way. Our problem today is not that you need to love Jesus more, but it's understanding and realizing how much He already loves you. It's why you need Him. Look at the happenings of King David:

> *Then King David went in and sat before the Lord and said, "Who am I, O Lord God, and what is my house, that you have brought me thus far?* -2 Samuel 7:18

The faith and trust of those Old Testament saints was unmatched. I say, a true saint of God is a true saint. Look in the New Testament and see Peter's character. We know he was aggressive, self-assertive, and self-confident. Did Jesus pick him because he had all the tools and qualities for leading others to a godly life? I don't think so. When Peter really saw Jesus, it's one of those first encounter stories where Peter had been fishing all night long and caught nothing. Jesus then said, *"Go back out, and put your nets out again."* He didn't want to because he was a proud fisherman, but he did it. The result was that they could barely haul the fish in. Here's Peter's response,

> *...he fell down at Jesus' knees, saying, "Depart from me, for I am a sinful man, O Lord."* -Luke 5:8

Poor in spirit is to recognize our sinfulness before the Holy God. Back in the Old Testament Isaiah got a glimpse of glory and said, "Woe is me!" Zip ahead again to the New Testament, and the Apostle

Paul spells it out for us, pointing out the attitude of the Jews who were uppity about being more religious than the common folks:

> *The very credentials these people are waving around as something special, I'm tearing up and throwing out with the trash—along with everything else I used to take credit for. And why? Because of Christ. Yes, all the things I once thought were so important are gone from my life. Compared to the high privilege of knowing Christ Jesus as my Master, firsthand, everything I once thought I had going for me is insignificant—dog dung. I've dumped it all in the trash so that I could embrace Christ and be embraced by him.*
>
> *-Philippians 3:7,8*

All these tremendous men of God and their testimonies of trust move us to understanding what it is to be poor in spirit. Compared to God, and He is our only true measurement, we are irrelevant — paltry waste. However, there is no better example for us to see than our Lord Himself, while the rest of America is busy trying to find out how to be rich and famous, big time with big money, and to fill our vaults with more and more. He took on the likeness of sinful man. He became a person, like us, and though He was equal with God He did not clutch at this prerogative of the Godhead. He emptied Himself. He decided that while He was on this planet that He would live like a man. He said, *"I can do nothing of myself."* Here are more of our Lord's words describing His person:

> *"Do you not believe that I am in the Father and the Father is in me? The words that I say to you I do not speak on my own authority, but the Father who dwells in me does his works."*   *-John 14:10*

Go further and look at His prayer life. The disciples asked, "Where is He?" They searched high and low for Him. It was mysterious. Where did He go for prolonged periods of time? He was with the Father, praying. Do you see the poverty of spirit?

Once more, let me put the question to you: What is poor in spirit? It's the emptying and absence of pride. It's the absence of self-confidence and self-reliance. Understand this, it means we are nothing in the presence of Almighty God and that we are very aware of it. Do you see how this flies in the face of modern culture? This is a provocation. The enemy incites our selfishness when we seek to be poor in spirit.

Everything this material world does is to lift man up to be exalted. We get our meaningfulness and self-worth from our work, our intellect, our education, our stacks of money, our reputation and notoriety, our stocks and bonds and portfolios. But discern this: when we get before Him, we can't and won't be able to produce something, anything, of substance. It's our utter nothingness that counts as we come face-to-face before the Holy God.

Here's your caveat: The true Christian, the real Christ-follower cannot rely on their natural birth. Just because you have a certain last name, a particular nationality, come from a specific nation — It's nothing before God. Before God, it's not your position in government, civic affairs, money, or trade. Paul said it's dung. That's right, dung. Dung smells. It's worthless, and in our world it's in mass abundance. The Greek word is found in a passage of Philippians, and it means garbage. You throw it out because it has no value. Now, do you understand the poverty of spirit? If you grasp the "dung" part, then you are close to being poor in spirit. It is to feel and know we are nothing, we have nothing, and we look to God in total submission and dependence. Again, it's Isaiah, 'Woe is me....' That's more of being poor in spirit.

Here's the big question: **How do I become poor in spirit?** You can't do it yourself. Fifteen hundred years ago the monks, those so-called holy men, tried to go the opposite way in being holy. Instead of collecting more piety, diplomas, money, positions of power, or religious prestige, they did the opposite and deprived themselves. That's how they defined holiness. There was one monk, in particular, who didn't bathe for over thirty years and when he died they couldn't distinguish his skin from his clothes. They had to scrape him up from where he'd sat for all those years. That's not poor in spirit, that's stupid and stinking in spirit.

My wife, Missie, is the real theologian in the family. As she read my notes on this manuscript, she asked, "Who do you think was the poorest in spirit in the Bible?" I hadn't really thought about it, and put the question back to her and said, "I don't know, who do you think?" She quickly responded, "The thief on the Cross!" (She was ready for me with her answer). "Yes! Yes!" I screamed.

He was hanging there, and he was morally bankrupt. He called out to Jesus because he was spiritually busted. The other thief, on the other side, mocked Jesus and said, "Aren't you the Christ! Save yourself and save us too!" But this thief, humble, poor, pitiful, and poor in spirit said, "Jesus, remember me when you come into your kingdom." And Jesus said to him, *"Truly, I say to you, today, you will be with me in paradise."* The thief on the Cross... yes, he never took communion, but he was poor in spirit. He was never baptized, but he was poor in spirit. He never even got to get on his knees to bow to King Jesus, but he was poor in spirit. There was absolutely nothing religious for the thief to do to physically prove he had emptied himself, but to exhale all his pride and sin.

The way to become poor in spirit is to look at God. Look at the Word of God because it causes us to look at Him. The more we look at Him the more we will respond like Jesus' disciples and cry out, *Lord, increase my faith!* They had been a part of healing the sick, and they realized they were nothing. They arrived at that point of being poor in spirit because they looked at Him for who He was and is. Look at Him and you will feel hopeless. Look at Him and you will feel worthless. Look at Him and you will see and know you are nothing without Him. Look at Him and you will become poor in spirit. Look at Him and keep looking at Him. Look at the saints that have gone before you. Look at that godly mother or father God put in your life. Look back to that God-seeking grandparent He provided you. Look at them all and realize His goal for your life has always been for you to be poor in spirit. But above all, look at Jesus again today. You can't look at Him without feeling absolute poverty and empty in spirit. And you can say,

Nothing in my hand I bring.
Simply to the Cross I cling...

It's His goodness in your life with you being empty. Pray this prayer, "God, I want to be with you every day, and I want be with you in eternity." Blessed are the poor in spirit, for theirs is paradise, for theirs is the kingdom of heaven.

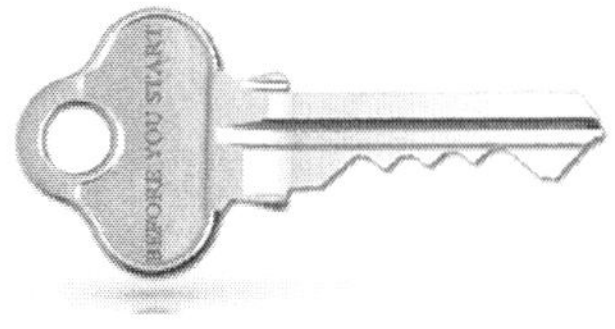

Attitude #2 · Start Crying

"Blessed are those who mourn, for they shall be comforted."
-Matthew 5:4

If you knew how quickly people would forget about you after your death, you will not seek in your life to please anyone but God.
-John Chrysostom

I like to laugh. I like light-hearted living, generally. I avoid stress. I gravitate towards the non-performance and spectacle life. I left the hallways of seventh grade drama a long time ago. What about you? I have catalogued in my brain the best laughter times I've ever experienced. I look forward to smiling as much as possible and enjoying life from here forward. The Bible says there is a time to cry and a time to laugh. Laughing is fun! It means we are happy or jovial. And that is why you can't just read the Beatitudes and say, "Well, how about that." A serious study of Jesus' Sermon prelude causes us to do deep inspection of our souls. It goes far beyond being light-hearted.

The Beatitudes is one of the most difficult passages in the Bible to interpret to our living. For an introduction to a sermon, these eight

13

expository statements are deeper than they appear on the surface. Too often, we like a soft opening to the pastor's message to put us at ease or get us in the mood to listen. Too many contemporary speakers approach the sermon as if they are on a stage for stand-up comedians. I have fallen into that trap too! If I were writing or suggesting some "Be" attitudes of daily living, then I would present something like this:

- Blessed are those who laugh a lot, they will enjoy life
- Blessed are those who smile, smile, smile, they will avoid crying
- Blessed are those who make others laugh, you will be liked
- Blessed are those who celebrate every minute, every day, they will avoid stress
- Blessed are those who seek happiness at any cost, they will not be sad

Are your beatitudes anything like that? I bet they are. Who would have ever thought about speaking or writing about your everyday attitude in this mundane world without including laughter? Jesus says nothing about amusement, hilarity, merriment, or glee. Nothing. As a matter of fact, there is absolutely nothing — nowhere recorded in Scripture — about Jesus laughing. Did Jesus laugh? You know He did. I'm sure He did. I think He did. I'm confident He laughed plenty about this crazy world and the people in it. I don't think He was mean spirited and made fun of people, but surely He laughed at our assumptions and the parodies of daily life.

The world's philosophy is to forget your troubles. The latter part of the Twentieth Century saw the rise of the comedy club. Now, we watch our favorite funny person online or on some streaming service. We also adhere to the adage: time heals all wounds. The institution of America is to be entertained. Leave your worries behind, go somewhere, drink away your problems, and drown your sorrows. But that's not what Jesus says happiness is, nor where you find it. It's not what the Gospels say either. All these Beatitudes are about our spiritual condition, or our spiritual attitude. Look at the words of our Lord again:

> *"Blessed are those who mourn, for they shall be comforted."*

Mourn! Mourn? Mourning is exactly what we want to avoid in our lives. Remember, when our grandparents used to reserve mourning for funerals? Remember these:

- They wore all black to symbolize our mourning and pain.
- They dressed up because it was a serious time.
- They had funerals in churches because it was the holy place for a holy time.
- They rode slowly in a parade of cars with their lights on, led by the unhurried hearse because they didn't want to rush it.
- They had wakes and visitation times the day before the funeral to talk and remember the dead with their endearing stories.
- And if you are old enough, maybe you remember when there was a time where they sat up with the dead. Yeah, they didn't want to leave them alone during the night before the funeral the next day… so people would sit up with the dead as they were laid out in the living rooms or in the parlor of the funeral home.
- They mourned because of the loss.
- They cried because of the pain of separation.
- They sobbed because of the heartache of not seeing their loved ones again. And they said, "Those were the good ol' days."

Not today. We've completely changed the mourning process when someone dies. For the sake of laughing instead of being sad, and for the exchange of smiles for tears, the funeral service is now referred to as a *celebration of life*. I understand, I get it. We do a lot of crying when we lose someone, and we want to change the somber mood and remember the happier times.

Rather than concentrating on healing our sadness, though, we need to see our attitudes. We've become flippant with God and that has altered our approach to Him, and just about everything else in our lives. Our world wants to live so much for ourselves that we will avoid thinking about death and what is to come. Most people are trying to duck and dodge the fact that we are all preparing for a judgment. At the same time, we are also trying to hold on to something we've always done, the way we've always done it, and keep things the same for as long as possible. And this "woke world" is catching up with us.

Our dismissive attitude with God is directly related to the fact that we sidestep sorrow. Think about it, especially men, we will do anything not to cry — particularly not in public! Here's my question to those who want to change the mourning to a party while at a funeral: What are you celebrating? Life? If you are celebrating the new life in Christ that culminates with eternity in glory, then I concur. Celebrate that life all the time. The Apostle Paul wrote to the Romans,

> *We know that our old self was crucified with him in order that the body of sin might be brought to nothing, so that we would no longer be enslaved to sin. For one who has died has been set free from sin.*　　　　　　　　　　*-Romans 6:6-7*

Now that's something to celebrate! However, if it's to raise a toast and get drunk to remember the party days with your long-gone friend Mickey, Tonya, Muffy, or Chip, then you don't have a clue what this Beatitude means. My friend, it is much more complex than that.

College football and basketball (and the rest of the college sports I suppose) has this ridiculous new thing called *entering the portal*. There was a time when, if you signed to play with a particular school, you committed to receiving a scholarship to that school and you continued your matriculation there to graduation. Not these days. You can change universities and colleges like you change your clothes. Commitment? What is that anymore? This process of changing schools is what is called *entering the portal.* They may define it as "exploring your options," but everybody knows what it really means. It means the athlete is unsatisfied with their current situation and is looking to take their talent elsewhere. At the best, it's an in-between time.

When you die you don't enter a portal, you go straight there... one place or the other... catch my drift? The religious portal is this world wishing, and hoping, that everything is just going to turn out all right by avoiding the truth.

I believe there is a huge movement to discard mourning from our society. Mourning doesn't fit the Western lifestyle. Maybe we are all looking for the portal of suspended time, where we don't have to commit. America has taken death and turned it into another reason to celebrate. It's exactly why Jesus didn't say, 'Blessed are those who laugh and party, for they will find Budweiser, and enjoy life!"

The great theologian, B.B. Warfield wrote a little book called, *The Emotional Life of our Lord.* Warfield's opening statement is footnoted to Calvin, "It belongs to the truth of our Lord's humanity, that he was subject to all sinless human emotions." Calvin said that those who do not believe in His humanity, and His human passions, don't really know Him. So, what do we do about emotional Jesus, and what is this second Beatitude all about?

Jesus Got Angry

There is no record of laughter in Jesus' life, but it doesn't mean He didn't laugh. What it does mean is that we desperately need to look at His emotions. We do know He got angry. It's black and white in Scripture:

> *And they were bringing children to him that he might touch them, and the disciples rebuked them. But when Jesus saw it, he was <u>indignant</u> and said to them, "Let the children come to me; do not hinder them, for to such belongs the kingdom of God."*　　　　　　　　　　　　　*-Mark 10:13-14*

To be indignant means to be enraged. It means to be angry — to be mad. This is a fantastic time in this book for me to remind those in church of our real ministry. Whatever it is you are doing in ministry at your church, whatever it is, move children to the top of your list. The ministry, in itself, is emotional. If you are parking cars on Sunday morning, make sure the children are safe. If you are in the production or technical part of the service — mark it down — if the children's equipment and production is not more important to you than putting the pastor's sermon online, then you are wrong and don't care about what Jesus cared about. If you are in leadership at your church and it's not the children you are thinking about, and how you can reach the children in your neighborhood, and how you can partner with entities and schools God placed beside you, then you are not thinking like God wants you to think for the church. Another example: If you are serving coffee on Sunday morning and your thought isn't, "What can we serve to the children," then you don't get it.

There is something to this emotional, angry side of Jesus in Scripture. Pause here and read it again. This poignant, passionate look at the Savior with children gives us a peek at His zeal for real life. And in a world that increasingly hates children... yeah, I said it. When we have American leaders who make abortion their number one goal and turn their heads as the gay community indoctrinates kids younger and younger and allows the bodily mutilation of elementary students in the name of transsexualism, then we hate children. Notice, I didn't mention child slavery and prostitution. Yeah, Jesus is angry.

Jesus was a man of sorrow

He was despised and rejected by men, a man of sorrows and acquainted with grief.
-Isaiah 53:3

There is a new television series called *The Chosen*. It's remarkable to interpret the New Testament as we thought it would look, and the characteristics and attitudes of people and what they must have really been like. But we need to be very careful and make sure TV interpretations don't dictate our theology. I love it that the series shows Jesus' emotions. He is depicted as humorous and fun-loving. It's cool, but Scripture is very clear and paints a total picture of our Lord that is often discarded. His visage, His face, was one of sorrow. I just don't think you would have lived two thousand years ago and seen Jesus walking down the road and said, "Oh! He looks like a happy God! I'll follow Him!" As a matter of fact, there is good, good reason to think that He looked older than he appeared. He was speaking to the Pharisees, and they said Abraham this and Abraham that, and look:

> *"Your father Abraham rejoiced that he would see my day. He saw it and was glad." So the Jews said to him, "You are not yet fifty years old, and have you seen Abraham?"*   *-John 8:56-57*

We know He's about thirty, thirty-one years old at most here. And they are saying He looks close to fifty? Hmmm. Reminder: never is it recorded that Jesus laughed. Maybe this is significant.

Jesus wept

It's the shortest verse in the Bible, John 11:35. *Jesus wept.* It wasn't because His best friend was dead that He wept. He was going there to raise him from the dead. And let me point out something: it surely wasn't a celebration of life. No, Jesus cried over something else. Look at Luke 19, Jesus is on the way to the Cross as He comes back into Jerusalem, It says,

> *When the city came into view, he wept over it. "If you had only recognized this day, and everything that was good for you! But now it's too late."*   *-Luke 19:41,42*

This is the picture of the Savior the Scripture paints for us. He is a man of sorrows. His look at this life is unlike our view. Notice how vastly different it is from what the so-called contemporary church teaches today. The Apostle Paul writes in Romans 7, "I do what I don't want to do...!" And, "I don't do what I should do...!" He then says,

Grasp this: All Christians are meant to be that way. A true Christian knows what it means to be utterly hopeless without Christ. Once more: *Blessed are those who mourn, for they will be comforted.* What does it mean? First, it follows being "poor in spirit." As I bow before God and His holiness, and contemplate the life I am meant to live, I must see myself as hopeless and helpless. I discover the deprived quality of my spirit and immediately it makes me mourn. This world cries for equity and equality when we are all equal in sin. We should mourn that we are like that, sinners. I don't know about you, but I'm sad when my spiritual structure falters and I collapse in sin. Why am I like that? Because I have been born into it like you.

Someone confronted me last week. They got in my face about this very subject. They said, 'No, you have to believe in yourself! It's the only way to be happy. You have to think positively. You have to say to yourself that you can do it!" Time out. I'm not saying we don't need to be positive, and try and set our standards and goals high, and work hard to achieve. I'm not saying that at all. We need to practice and run hard the race of life. What Jesus is saying to us is to be real, and to really look at life. To, at some point, call our own timeout, step back, and look hard at life. If you must, go into the locker room and regroup at the halftime of your life. You are born on a certain date, and you will expire on a certain date. To the person who says, "All you have to do is to dig deep and believe in yourself and you will be successful, I don't need God," my selfish self wants to respond in a smart-aleck way,

"Good luck!" But, when we truly mourn the condition of this society, we beg God to rescue them.

Let me ask you something. Have you seen Arnold Schwarzenegger with his shirt off lately? In the 70's he had this ultimate buff body that won him Mr. Olympia eight times. He's now an old man. To the person who says I can live to 120 and I'm going to live it out at the beach, live it up in the city, and live all my days burning the candle at both ends: have you talked to someone whose parents have dementia lately? When was the last time you visited a nursing home? Just go and observe for five minutes, and inquire what life is like. To the "I can do it" crowd, have you seen someone who is ninety-five years old try to run a mile? There might be a few on this planet who can do it, but it doesn't look like those thoroughbreds who line up at the starting line at the Olympics.

Here's what we should do as Christ-followers: take inventory every night as you lay your head on the pillow and ask, *What have I done, what have I said, and what have I thought today?* Guess what? Chances are every other day, once a week, every day maybe, you've violated your commitment to God. You've lied to God. You left your first love, as the church in Ephesus did. You've cheated God. You've lied to yourself. Perhaps you've cheated others. Maybe you've figured out things aren't as you thought.

And then, after those condemning thoughts, there comes the enemy with his fix-it plan and says, *"believe in yourself, be positive, laugh more and lighten up and things are going to work out, you'll see."* How's that going for you? Then you realize that the Christian is smitten with grief, and sorrow too. But get this: you can't stop there. You need to take inventory of your life and ask, "Why? Why do I act like that? Why do I respond like I do? Why do I use that language, and have that attitude, and make those comments? Why am I jealous, envious, and unkind? Why? What is in me?" And if you don't mourn over that then you are not blessed, as Jesus puts it. And if you think it's just life, and who you are, then you are not the spiritual soul and soldier of Christ.

Wait! The Christian doesn't stop there either. The Christ-follower sees their friends, and the hurt and pain in their lives, and mourns, and prays for them, and seeks to encourage them in the name of Jesus. We go even further and see the pain and unrest in the world. The rumor of war, crime, death on the street, drugs in our neighborhoods and schools, the ruining of our country's once held values, and we could go on and on. Jesus' weeping was because of that. He saw the progression of sin. He saw that the enemy wants to steal, kill, and destroy. He knew Satan will not stop at making you trip and fall every few years. I learned a long time ago,

Sin costs you more than you want to pay
Sin takes you farther that you want to go
Sin keeps you longer than you want to stay

Jesus mourned at sin. He was called to the grave of Lazarus, and He wept over the outcome of sin. He saw this ugly, horrid, foul thing, and it introduced death to life, and made life unhappy, difficult, and painful. Later, on His walk to the Cross, He approached Jerusalem, with hundreds of years of history of God saying, "I will be your God and you will be my people." The Bible records promise after promise, and multiple covenants given by the Father, and now we look at the worldliness of His Holy city. We can survey the forgetfulness and offensiveness of His chosen people. That is why He wept and cried. It grieved Him. And we are told, "He is a man of sorrows, and acquainted with grief."

Mourning is the antithesis, the complete opposite, of how this world wants us to think. We are at war within ourselves, and the enemy's answer is to eat buffet and gourmet style. It's to get filled up on drink. It's to indulge in drugs to forget about it. You got troubles? Do you see it, the world says, "Laugh more!" "Grab life with gusto more!" "Collect, save, and make more!" Jesus says, *"Lose it all and you will find ME."* We mourn over the wrong thing when we cry over losing our stuff, instead of making it our lifelong desire to lose more of what this world describes as success. If you don't know this, maybe it will help: The way of the Lord is always the complete opposite way of this world. Jesus tells us that happiness (*how can this be?)* is found in mourning. The sinner must hate sin. The Christian is to grieve over it because it is the highest stinking offense to our God, and He grieves over it. He mourns over it — yet He forgives sin!

That's it, Pastor? We are to just keep on mourning? Crying all the time and to be sad every day — doesn't this paint a gloomy picture of being a Christian? To weep. Wail. Seriously, that's it? Happiness is mourning? That's what you are telling me? No, not quite. The blessing, the happiness is in the comfort. Again,

> *"Blessed are those who mourn, for they shall be comforted."*

The person who mourns over their sin is going to turn their life around. It will never be the person who goes on thinking they've got it all handled. Never. And the person who repents and turns their life around is the real person the Holy Spirit is working in and through. When we see our utter failure before a righteous God, then we will turn around, and seek the Savior, Christ our Lord. The truly astounding thing about the Christian life is that your great sorrow leads to great joy. Jesus says, "You are blessed."

Who is this person who mourns? What kind of person are they? It's not just at conversion, but it's continual in your journey with Christ. This person is sorrowful, but not miserable. This person is serious, but not solemn. This person has a grave knowledge of this world but is not cold. No, they look at life differently from the rest of this world. They see the sin, they see the effects, and they are serious about life rather than trying to escape it. The Christian life is a deep doctrine of sin, and a high doctrine of joy. Because there comes a day when the comfort the Bible promises is *no more tears.* That's what heaven is: no more sorrow. Those who have rejected Christ are trying to create their heaven on earth by avoiding tears, because that is the best they will ever have. But one day there will be no more demands of sin. The disobedience to God will be gone. Life will be perfect, again.

As I write this, I am aware that many people, and I'm talking about the people in church, are swimming in sin. People in my church and your church are drowning in disobedience and confusion in knowing Jesus today. He knows it. He wants to bless you today and the blessing — oh the blessing — is in the comfort. Jesus is speaking about life in the Kingdom in the Beatitudes. He's not talking about you adding Him to your life for a few jollies and goosebumps every now and then. He is the God who is there, but we keep running from our problems and disobedience thinking that one day we are just going to fix it, or maybe it will work out. It won't. That is why the answer to your troubles right now is to mourn for your sin, and He will give you comfort.

In Daniel 2, in the Old Testament, King Nebuchadnezzar had a dream that disturbed him. He demanded that his wise men, his magicians, those astrologers of his, tell him what he dreamed and what it meant. They gathered and they broke the news to old king Neb, and he didn't like it. He said, "If you don't interpret my dream, then I'm going to tear you limb from limb and bulldoze your house." And so, after they failed, Neb issued a law to kill all the wise men in the land. All of them — no matter who they were. Daniel and the Hebrew Three (Shadrach, Meshach, and Abednego) had been taken captive from Judah and were prisoners. They were going to be killed too. Daniel told the three to pray for him. Daniel spoke to the general who had been given the order to kill the wise men and said, "Get me an audience with the king." Daniel walked in, and King Nebuchadnezzar says, "Are you the one who is going to make known my dream and interpret it?" And Daniel said, "No". "No, king, I'm not. And neither will any of your wise men, nor your astrologers, nor your enchanters, nor your magicians." Then Daniel made this powerful statement that rings true even today, and will forever:

"But there is a God in heaven..."

Perhaps the weight of the world in on your shoulders right now, and it looks like your entire livelihood is about to fold up, but there is a God in heaven. Maybe it's the end of the rope for you, it looks like there is no hope, and you feel you just can't go on — there is a God in heaven. The pain and suffering and hurt are too much to bear, there is a God in heaven. The tears, oh my, the tears, they are flooding your eyes and you've cried so much you are just sick of crying, and sick of talking about the pain. My friend, there is a God in heaven who knows — He sees — and He wants to change your life. He will change your life. He will make your grave into a garden. He will make your old dry bones come alive. There is a God in heaven, and when we mourn for our sin, then we can be comforted by Him.

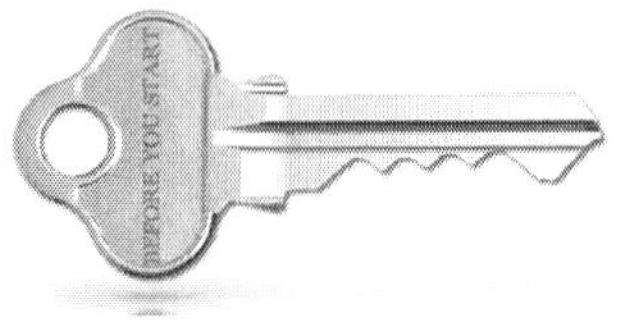

Attitude #3 • Seek Meek

"Blessed are the meek, for they shall inherit the earth."

-Matthew 5:5

I simply taught, preached, and wrote God's Word; otherwise, I did nothing. The Word did everything.   -Martin Luther

Abortion and infanticide were signed into law, and racism was at its highest point. When your enemy wants to kill you, it's the most critical point. The King of Egypt issued a decree that all Hebrew boys born must be murdered on demand. That was by his command. It wasn't until Pharaoh, King of Egypt, deputized every Egyptian citizen to hate the Jews, that they controlled their population. And his command was, if you found one, throw him into the river Nile. You see, Pharaoh had tried to get the midwives, those delivering the Hebrew babies, to secretly kill the boys who were born. But surreptitiously they were letting them live. And there was one woman who, for some reason — well, you know the reason — she was a mom. She was willing to go to extraordinary lengths. She hid her newborn son until he could be hidden no longer.

You can't blame the Levite woman, Moses' mom. She obeyed the law. She threw her son into the river, just as the law required. She did take some liberties, though. She threw him into the Nile in a basket. She had waterproofed the wicker container with bitumen (tar, or pitch) to ensure the safety of her son. And she gently floated it down the river at a time when she knew the daughter of Pharaoh was bathing. Irony, isn't it? Pharaoh says throw them in the river to rid the world of God's people, and God throws a boy into the river to rescue His people.

The infant boy was found by Pharoah's daughter, and he grew up in the palace. More than likely, the princess created a word using a combination of Egyptian and Hebrew, thus the name Moses. It means *to draw out of*, the Bible says, because they drew him out of the water. What do you think you get when you grow up in the palace of the most powerful man on the planet? Of course, you get everything and anything your heart desires. When you get everything in this world, you begin to live as if the world is about you. When you get anything in this world, you begin to live like you are the center of creation. Many people do that today.

Moses inhabited his environment and world. He was the prince of Egypt; we see it in Exodus chapter two. As prince, he had everything and anything at his fingertips. He was in the ultimate position to wield control over a people. Despite this, the Bible says, he was the meekest — the meekest on the planet. However, it's not a description given to him early in Exodus chapter three. No, his meekness was not revealed until later, in chapter twelve of the Old Testament book of Numbers. That was forty years later.

Here's the point to knock you off your rocker: NO ONE IS BORN MEEK. Meek isn't always on our radar and probably not what you are thinking about today. Then why is it chapter three of this book? God wants you and every believer to live a meek life. Modern day Christianity and so-called contemporary churches are full of motivational talks of how to be bold for Jesus. We are inundated with talks of turning things up in our lives. They say things like, "Turn up the music, turn up your walk, be loud and turn up your faith for Jesus so you can receive more and more!" Present day theology is that your faith can make you healthy, so you can get rich, and if you are rich, then you can be happier. In chapter three of this book, we've already discovered that Jesus' way, the life God wants us to live, is so antithetical, so opposite, to how this world says for us to live. Additionally, many churches, Christian organizations, and mission societies are way off base.

Open any newspaper, turn to any news cycle and you will find that China, Russia, Iran, North Korea, are into world conquest and domination. Wall Street, the New York Stock Exchange, and Shanghai are jockeying for financial positions. The philosophy of the world is that for success, you must keep ascending to the top! Yet the Christian life is different from this world and does not at all fit this mold.

When you are in Christ you are a new person, a new creation the Bible says, and you are not of this world. The faith that is in you is put there by God. It is alien to this world. The Christian life consists of God transforming you and me. I don't know about what kind of life change you have heard about before, or expect in Jesus, but I'm certain it's not to come to church and get your religion on. Not only is this world unlike Him. This outside, liberal world, does not understand Him. And if you are not a problem, an enigma, to those around you who are not Christians, then that says something about you.

It is something profound that the Lord Jesus preaches this sermon to you, and He began it with some things you need to apply to your life before you think about starting the Christian life — even if you have to renew and begin again today. God melted that worldly heart of Moses, and it took forty years. Again, here's what God says to us,

> *"Blessed are the meek, for they shall inherit the earth."*   *-Matthew 5:5*

Apart from the Lord Jesus, the Bible proclaims only one other person as meek. And yet, our God wants you to be meek. I'm not joking — He doesn't expect anything less. Moses was described as meek in the Old Testament book of Numbers. Plenty could have the modifier of meekness, but only Moses besides the Lord Jesus is described in words as meek. We deduce that Abraham was meek. Abraham and his nephew Lot had to split up because they couldn't share land anymore, their flocks were too big. Abraham said to Lot, "You choose. Wherever you want to go, you choose first."

David was surely meek to an extent. He started out as just a shepherd boy. He was the runt of the family. However, one day He was anointed king by the prophet Samuel on God's command. But it was a secret in the beginning. It wasn't yet time because other things had to fall into place first. David didn't try to hunt down Saul, dispose of him, and take over early. Rather, David respected God's timing.

Stephen, that fiery preacher in the book of Acts was meek in the final scene of his life. He stood boldly in front of God-haters and preached the Gospel of Jesus Christ and, as they stoned him to death, he begged God to forgive them. That's being meek.

What is Meekness?

First thing, one more time (at least), you aren't born with it. No one is born meek. Yet every Christ-follower is called to be meek. Every Christian is being transformed to a state of meekness. Look throughout Scripture and it's the one thing every God-fearer became. This Beatitude is not reserved for the preachers or missionaries or the super-saints. It's for you! This Beatitude is not set aside for the serious Bible student only — nor are any of the rest of them. Do you see the progression of the Beatitudes so far? It begins with the *Poor in Spirit*, emptying ourselves of our pride. Then, we need to mourn over the fact of our sin and disobedience to the Holy God. And now, meekness. What is it?

Here's what it's not:

- **Laziness** – Some people give the appearance of meekness by their slothful living but that's not meekness, it's just being lazy.
- **Flabbiness** – Meekness is not sitting around and reading the Bible 24/7, even though that would do a lot of us good. We tend to think that if someone is easygoing then they are meek. That's not what Jesus is talking about.

I like the Message translation of this verse in 1 Timothy:

> *Stay clear of silly stories that get dressed up as religion. Exercise daily in God— no spiritual **flabbiness**, please! Workouts in the gymnasium are useful, but a disciplined life in God is far more so, making you fit both today and forever.*
> *-1 Timothy 4:7,8 [The Message]*

Spiritual flabbiness means *faking it*. But the fake-acting, and Christian spiritual flabbiness, will find you out. Let the normal rigors of life happen to you while living a counterfeit relationship with Jesus, while living a lazy Christian life, and see what happens. It's not pretty.

- **Niceness** – Your dog is nice. It's not what Jesus is talking about either. Some people, because of their environment, because of how they grew up with great parents, are nice. But you need to know that what Jesus is talking about is not something that comes naturally to anyone. Remember, no one is born meek.
- **Weakness** – Weakness is not meekness. How often, in the middle of a skirmish, and the verbal blows are tossed, and someone stands up and says, "Let's just get along and try to be nice and kind and happy." And we think, "Oh, that's meek!" No, meekness is comparable to great strength. The martyrs, those who have been murdered for their belief in Christ, were meek but not weak.
- **Outwardness** – No, it's innerness. Meekness is not only resisting putting up your dukes, but also silencing your mouth.

You can't spend time on this verse, spewing it on others and rubbing it in, without it humbling and changing you. **Meekness is true Christianity**. I know many have been fooled into thinking true Christians are the ones driving new Cadillacs, who have no problems, and no health risks. The truth is, meekness is a major characteristic of the Christ-follower. *Blessed are the meek* – this is what we are called to, it's what we were meant to be!! So, what is meekness?

Meekness is a TRUE, VIEW of YOU, expressing YOU (Attitude & Conduct) with respect to others

Get these two things: your attitude towards yourself, and your expression in relationship to others. It's looking in the mirror and seeing who God says we are — and without Him, we see we are nothing. It's massively important to recognize the order in which Jesus puts these Beatitudes. Let's review: You can't be meek without first being poor in spirit. Poor in spirit is emptying yourself. It's the absence of pride, getting rid of the notion of *"*I can do it myself.*"Blessed are those who mourn* is next. It's a mourning of our sinfulness, it's lamenting the person we should have been prior to giving our lives to Christ and following Him in obedience. It is the mourning of the state of the world and of society. The meek are not proud of themselves. Let's put it plain Jane, here's meekness:

#1 You don't care about expressing yourself

In a world where the name of the game is cutting and editing our video to go on TikTok or Facebook, we love to plaster our names all over the place. We feel that it makes us somebody. When we are recognized, and others show us attention, then we feel important and needed.

I realize I am revealing my age, but have you seen that scene in the movie, *The Jerk,* when Navin R. Johnson, played by Steve Martin, gets a phone book? The new phone book arrived, and he was giddy with excitement. As he searched and found his name he screamed with glee, "I am somebody!"

Let me explain this to everyone under forty. You see, before the Internet it was a big deal when the new phone book came out. It had your phone number in there (still not impressed?). People could look up your number and call you. You would see your name in print (that was important to us). We wanted to be somebody! Well, the meek person doesn't demand anything for themselves. The meek doesn't care about being somebody, they are into glorifying somebody else. They don't make demands because of position, possessions, privileges, or status in life. He is the person the Apostle Paul talks about in Philippians,

Think of yourselves the way Christ Jesus thought of himself.   *-Philippians 2:5*

How did Christ think of Himself? Paul says, He was in the form of God, He was equal with God, but He emptied Himself out. He humbled Himself to the point of death.

#2 You're not sensitive about yourself

Go back to the Garden in Genesis and you will see this lingering curse and the effect of the fall. It's the sensitivity of ourselves. We spend the whole time of our lives watching ourselves. If the mirror wasn't a bad enough primitive invention, then current social media has taken it to levels of destruction. When someone becomes meek, they are finished with all that sensitivity. They don't worry about themselves and what people say. To be truly meek is to not worry about protecting themselves, because there is nothing worth defending. The truly meek never pity themselves. He or she isn't sorry for himself/herself. They never say, "You are having a hard time and people are being unkind to you and they don't understand you." They never think, "How wonderful I am." It's never, "If they only gave me a chance." Hours and hours of our lives are wasted in our own sensitivity over what other people think about us. To be meek is to move far beyond that. The great Puritan writer, John Bunyan, said this, 'He that is down need fear no fall.'' Go ahead and realize that without Christ we are nothing anyway, and our job is to decrease while making Him increase.

#3 You're amazed God and others think of you and treat you as well as they do

Take off your goody-goody makeup, and your desire to put on the appearance that you are a Christ-follower. Don't pretend it — *be* a Christ-follower! Maybe, you need to start to be real in Christ, not the reality of the person only your spouse and kids see. Who is the real person you see in the mirror? Meekness is when we are shaken for our faults, to where we are corrected by God. It's when He allows us to go through the difficult junk and we go through the problematic stuff. And when we learn to go through it patiently — that is meekness.

Meekness always implies a teachable spirit. It's what we see in the Savior, of the Lord Jesus Himself. Though He was the second person in the blessed Holy Trinity, He became a man. He deliberately humbled Himself to the extent that He was entirely dependent upon what God gave Him. It's what God taught, and what God told Him to do. He humbled Himself, and that is being meek. Christian, hear me, we must be ready to learn and listen and especially surrender ourselves to the Spirit of God to walk in meekness.

#4 You leave EVERYTHING in the hands of God

We learn with the Apostle Paul, *"Vengeance is mine, says the Lord, I will repay."* Condemnation is not our job. Meekness is finally getting to that place where you let God handle things in your life. The more of Scripture I personally read, the more I see it telling me to wait on God. Waiting with hope in God is a great definition of meekness.

When we are meek, Jesus says, we have inherited the earth. Exactly what have we inherited? *Blessed are the meek, for they shall inherit the earth.* It means this: Someone who is truly meek is always satisfied. The person that is meek is content. It's having nothing, while having it all! There was an old gospel quartet song from the 1970's, by the group, The Kingsmen, called *Shake Hands With A Poor Boy.* Here's a part of the first verse:

> I've never had much, in this world below
> But I'm going to a city, where the streets are pure gold.
>
> Christ made me an heir; I'm the child of a king
> Shake hands with a poor boy, who owns everything.

My friends, that's meekness. Paul wrote to the Corinthians to help them sort things out and to live the Christian life. He says,

> *We are treated as impostors, and yet are true; as unknown, and yet well known; as dying, and behold, we live; as punished, and yet not killed; as sorrowful, yet always rejoicing; as poor, yet making many rich; as having nothing, yet possessing everything.*   *-2 Corinthians 6:8-10*

When we realize that we own everything, and have everything we need in Christ, then we are meek. Paul wrote to the church at Philippi, and in the conclusion he was thanking them for their financial gift. He really appreciated it. And this verse describing the gentleness and meekness of Paul has become to mean the exact opposite in our culture:

> *I rejoiced in the Lord greatly that now at length you have revived your concern for me. You were indeed concerned for me, but you had no opportunity. Not that I am speaking of being in need, for I have learned in whatever situation I am to be content. I know how to be brought low, and I know how to abound. In any and every circumstance, I have learned the secret of facing plenty and hunger, abundance and need. I can do*

Paul is basically saying, *thanks for the money, but Jesus is all I really need.* He doesn't need the money to do church, to preach the Gospel, or to live for Jesus. If he was hungry, suffering, and poor, Paul says, *"God strengthens me to do all things."* That is meekness. Paul also tells Timothy, *"Don't worry about your suffering Tim, be meek, and suffer, and you will reign with Him."* Jesus describes meekness in the parable of the wedding feast. He says, if you are invited to a wedding feast, don't assume that you are the most important person there, thinking you must rush to the best spot at the table. He tells us to let the host direct us where to sit, and we will be honored. Then, He gives us this meek verse:

You can't make yourself meek. Only the Holy Spirit can do that. Do you know what I find most interesting in this crazy modern day preaching and teaching? There is a lot of emphasis on being filled with the Holy Spirit. And we should, and you can be. But so many preachers are talking about being filled with the Spirit for boldness, for might, for strength, for miracles; for standing up tall for God, for executing impossible-looking ministry, for doing daring mission work, and on and on. But rarely, if ever, have I heard anyone want to be filled with the Spirit to be meek. Have you?

Here's a good question: How serious am I, on a scale of one to ten, about being meek to God? An eleven. If I were you today, reading this chapter, here's what I would do (because I did it already): I would call an emergency meeting with God. Don't put it off until tomorrow or next week. Today, now! It is that important. I would humble myself and confess my inadequacies. I would confess my disobedience and dishonoring of Him. I would confess sin that is hidden from the rest of the world. I would truly look in the mirror, to my soul, and ask myself if I was being honest with God. Meekness to God is not a show. It's the life He wants you to live on both the inside and the outside. In this meeting, I would confess my imperfections and I would ask Him to possess me wholly, totally, and completely. And then I would get on with the rest of my life.

My wife and I named our church FRESH. We are simply Fresh Church. Its basis is in Romans 6:4. Paul reminds us that in Christ, when we identify with Him, buried with Him in baptism, we are raised again to walk in newness of life. The Greek word for newness also means *fresh*. And in preparing this chapter, I found a new verse to bring validity and meaning to Fresh Church. Friends, it's always cool to discover the name of your church in Scripture:

> *The* **meek** *shall obtain fresh joy in the Lord...*
> *-Isaiah 29:19*

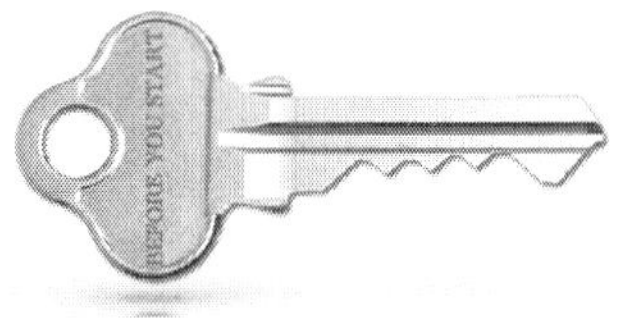

Attitude #4 • Hungry & Thirsty

"Blessed are those who hunger and thirst for righteousness, for they shall be satisfied." -Matthew 5:6

Nobody stood by Jesus. Maybe nobody will stand by you. It's a lonely life, but it's a glorious life. -Leonard Ravenhill

There seems to me to be many people who go from church to church, convention to convention, concert to concert, always hoping to get filled up spiritually. They are looking for some wonderful experience at a big concert coliseum that will satisfy them with joy and purpose, flooding them with ecstasy. They see that other people have it, but they don't get it. So, they seek it in a feeling, they covet it with their ears and eyes, and they are always thirsting and hungering for it, but they never get it. Is that you?

In Matthew 5 Jesus climbed a mountain with hundreds, perhaps thousands, following. The mountain slope provided an instant arena or Amphitheatre, where He could be heard better, and the people were comfortable in getting closer. He began to talk about the characteristics of a Christian. Be *Poor in Spirit,* or empty yourself. We learned previously that you must start there. The second Beatitude was a difficult one for us as Jesus says, *"Blessed are those who mourn, for they shall be comforted."* It's not just blubbering over spilt milk, that missed-out promotion, breaking up with your boyfriend, or even crying over someone who has died. It's about mourning over the sin in your life and how you have disobeyed God. More in review, the last chapter saw us look at the third Beatitude from Jesus: *Blessed are the meek, for they will inherit the earth.* Meekness is not a blank look on your face. It's not solemnity or even being quiet. Meekness is being real with yourself rather than trying to be someone you aren't, or to promote yourself. It's your Christ-like attitude towards yourself and one expressed to others.

This fourth attitude Jesus introduces is even deeper and more complex than the previous one. Yet it may be the one you are looking for. If you have been searching for the meaning of life, then splash your face with some water, sit up straight, pay attention, and give me about fifteen minutes because this could be the massive message you've been praying for. The word we are going to dwell on is my favorite word in the world. I just love to say it, especially while I am preaching and teaching. It's a religious word — sort of. It's a descriptive word. It's a wonderful word for us:

RIGHTEOUSNESS

"Blessed are those who hunger and thirst for righteousness, for they shall be satisfied."
-Matthew 5:6

If Matthew 5:6 is your favorite verse in the Bible, then I would probably say you are surely a Christian, without ever meeting you. Conversely, you will be sadly disappointed, disillusioned, and confused if you spend your time looking to be blessed materially or looking for a feeling-type experience with God. If you want to be happy in this life and live the Christian life, make sure you pay attention.

40

Have you ever thought of the thousands and thousands, the millions and millions, of dollars you have gone through looking for happiness? Not everyone reading this has had millions, but some have. You've spent it, maybe you've spent it all. Maybe you are entering the twilight of your life, and you just can't believe you haven't realized truth or happiness or meaningfulness.

If you want to be happy in this life and want to truly know what it means to be blessed, then you must do what Jesus says: *to hunger and thirst for righteousness.* The blessings, the happiness and joy, and the experiences with God, are what come from the pursuit of righteousness. It's sort of a byproduct.

What is righteousness? It's simply right living.

Live right is the answer to your problems. Live according to God and His Holy Word and you will never be bewildered. Did you think there was some secret code of ethics that we are to gravitate towards? Or some religious morals that we couldn't quite understand? There is no time like the present for you to start getting serious about living for God. The Lord Jesus says we are to hunger and thirst and covet right living. But hold on — before you consider righteousness in your everyday living, we have to talk about being able to stand in front of God, face to face in righteousness.

The term *righteous* is recorded approximately 287 times in Scripture. It's one thing to talk about being righteous when you are talking about being a Christ-follower, but it's another thing altogether when you talk about coming to Christ and getting right with God. God's purpose is to make you *justified* before Him. This justification, or salvation, means that you must be perfect. That's what the text says — *perfect.* God demands perfection, and He commands total righteousness. No one slips into His presence. No one gets a free pass. No one knows someone working the door who lets them slide by with a wink.

Our God must be sick and tired of the cheap grace that is offered up in our churches these days. False teachers and preachers have made God into a robotic toy. Using their bargain basement rhetoric, they program their listeners by saying, "God loves you unconditionally... just give your life to Him... and come and serve and give, and you will begin to be infused with His presence and one day it will all come to you."

Here's the truth: God doesn't love us unconditionally. There are conditions. You can't do whatever you want and still be perfect in Him. Those are two different lifestyles. Life in Christ isn't an introductory five-minute ceremony experienced at the end of a church service. Just because you cry crocodile tears doesn't mean that all is forgiven. You may have signed up, joined up, and 'fessed up, but a little offering of your time and money doesn't mean that God has said, "Congratulations! You've passed the test! You're a member!"

The word righteous means one thing to you and me — it means we are in serious trouble. The word picture in the New Testament is one of hopelessness. We don't have a shot at things turning out right, neither do we have a chance, and there is no hope, except in Christ Jesus. There is a holy God out there, and right where you are sitting, and He demands perfection. You don't have the liberty of one cuss word, not one little lie, and not a single cross word. Mean thoughts are not allowed, even in Jesus' name. You don't have permission to tell blatant lies or perform deceiving maneuvers. All vengeful actions, fraudulent transactions, deceptive and devious scheming, are things you gave up when you turned to Christ. Not to mention those eyes that have wandered, those feet that have fled... and that mouth, oh, that mouth. How many times have you denied God and denied Him working in your life. Let me say it so that you perfectly understand perfection. Everyone has sinned and fallen woefully short of God's standard, and the Bible doesn't pull any punches despite the goody-goody world we live in that yearns to soften the blow.

YOU AND I DON'T HAVE A SHOT. IT'S IMPOSSIBLE WITHOUT CHRIST BEING OUR PERFECTION FOR US.

> *For by works of the law <u>no human being will be justified in his sight</u>, since through the law comes knowledge of sin.*
>
> *But now the **righteousness of God** has been manifested apart from the law, although the Law and the Prophets bear witness to it—**the righteousness of God** through faith in Jesus Christ for all who believe.*   -Romans 3:20-22

Is it sinking in? There is a kingdom, a beautiful, gorgeous kingdom that is beyond our description. All your creativity and images of beauty don't come close to helping you paint the picture. It's reserved and exclusive. It's so unlike this world. In it, the KING presides and rules and reigns. He is a just KING. The Psalmist proclaims the throne of God has righteousness and justice as it's foundation. There was an old television detective show in the 1970's and the main character had the pat line, "if you do the crime, you do the time." The only problem is that there is no parole, the time is forever. And since we've all sinned, we're all doomed.

But He's not only just, He's also merciful. He knows you. He knows the power of sin and the lies of the enemy. He knows you live in a body that is wasting away. He knows it all. He knows your suffering and pain. He knows. He knows you want things to change, but you can't do enough good even if you did ten thousand good things a day for a hundred years. So, He provides a way. Acts 9 tells us that the new movement of Christianity was referred to, by those looking to destroy the early followers, as *"the Way."* Jesus is the Way to God's way of right living for your life. He gave us His Son, as *perfection* as the New Testament book of Romans says, and this righteousness He demands comes via trust, or what we call faith. Faith is devotion. Faith is change. Faith is trusting even when you can't see the invisible God. That is righteousness in salvation.

There is another righteousness that flows beautifully from Christ who rescued us. Righteousness leads to freedom. It's wanting to live free from sin because sin separates us from God. All the problems in the world today stem from a world that is not right with God. That is the teaching of the Bible. The person who hungers and thirsts after righteousness is the person who understands that sin and rebellion have separated them from the face of God. That person longs to get to that first relationship, that original relationship of total righteousness, that we witness in the Garden of Eden in Genesis 1 & 2. It is the desire to be free from the power of sin. And it goes even further than that.

The person who allows the Holy Spirit to examine their life in the illumination of the Scripture not only discovers that sin holds people in bondage as slaves, but that it's more horrible than we can imagine. As our society befriends sin it discovers it likes it. The more you stay in sin, the more you will deny it even exists. Even after discovering sin kills — it's remarkable but — we still do it! Even after finding out that sin separates us from God, we still engage in it. Further, after realizing the path of destruction it takes us down, we continue down that very same path.

The hunger and thirst for righteousness is simply and positively the longing to be holy. To hunger and thirst for righteousness is to hate sin. The person who hungers and thirsts for righteousness is the person who wants to exemplify the Beatitudes in their life. To hunger and thirst for righteousness is to be the New Testament person in Christ. It means to want to know God and to walk with God, and to be in fellowship with God. You may say, "I want that, but I am so far away from that, I just don't know if I can do it." The Apostle Paul knew those words you are saying,

> *Not that I have already obtained this or am already **perfect**, but I press on to make it my own, because Christ Jesus has made me his own.*   *-Philippians 3:12*

Press on and look at Him. Look at Him and His portrait in the Gospels. Look at Him when He walked this earth in the Incarnation — when God became like us. Look at Him in His positive obedience to God's Holy law. Look at Him as He preached this Sermon on that mountain and He says, *"Ask, and it will be given to you; seek, and you will find; knock, and it will be opened to you."* He insists that we persist in our walk with Him. Look at Him and His reaction to other people. His kindness, His compassion, and His sensitive nature are all on display in genuine love in Matthew, Mark, Luke, and John. Look at Him in His reaction to His enemies and all that they did to Him. He said, *"Father, forgive them, they don't know what they are doing."* There is a picture of righteousness in the New Testament, and for all those who have been born again to Jesus the supreme desire is to be like Christ.

What is the longest you have ever gone without food? I haven't missed many meals in my day. I don't know what it is to be truly hungry. How long have you gone without water? I was in the Egyptian desert once and went an entire day without water. Eight hours on camelback, and when I got to the traditional site of Mt. Sinai there was a pump well. I grabbed that pump handle and pumped and pumped until cold water flowed out of that well and I drank until I was full. I remember that day well. When they told me about the pump and the cold water — I had never pumped water before. But let me tell you, I learned how in thirty seconds. I was desperate. I was thirsty.

Recently, I traveled to the Holy Land with a group of friends. While we were there I was talking with my friends, Arnie and Becky Cribb, who had previously been on my team to start a church twenty-five years ago. Becky remarked, *"Pastor, you don't remember it, but three years ago you challenged people to read a Psalm or two every morning. I did it. Now, I have to do it every morning."* It's all about hungering and thirsting for God. Spiritual hunger and thirst are something deep and profound until they are satisfied.

There is always a great hunger and thirst in love. The chief desire of the one who loves is to be with the one they love. If they are separated there is no rest until they are together again. Do you know Psalm 42:

As a deer pants for flowing streams, so pants my
soul for you, O God.
My soul thirsts for God, for the living God.
-Psalm 42:1-2

These opening verses mean *to crave God.* J.N. Darby, an Irish preacher of two hundred years ago said, "To hunger is not enough, you must be starving." That is what Jesus means. Darby goes on to say that when the Prodigal son was hungry, he went in and ate the husks that the pigs had left over. But when he was starving, he went home to his father. To hunger and thirst for righteousness is to be desperate. It is to feel that life is ebbing out, and only He can satisfy. Here are some practicals:

#1 Avoid **EVERYTHING** opposed to Righteousness

#2 Actively **REMIND** yourself of Righteousness

#3 Always put yourself in the **WAY** of Righteousness

#4 Again, and again **READ** your **BIBLE**

#5 Awaiting you every day is **PRAYER**

#6 Awaken and be **ENCOURAGED** by the Righteous lives of others

Blessed are those who hunger and thirst for righteousness, for they will be filled. The whole of the Gospel is contained in this verse. God's salvation is a gift. You can't earn your way into heaven or into the good graces of God. He's given it to you, but you must receive it. Hold Up! Receiving is not simply praying a little prayer. Rather, it's the beginning of hungering and thirsting for right living in your life. When you turn to Him, He comes into your life. If you believe that Jesus died for your sin, you have been forgiven. No need to keep asking, now it's time to start living like it. The Christian should know if they are forgiven. If you never hunger and thirst for righteousness, then you will never have it. This one statement by our Lord Jesus sums up the whole doctrine of salvation and sanctification.

The people who hunger and thirst after righteousness are frantic people. They may go to concerts and raise their hands in worship. They may attend with zeal all the church growth conferences, and they may go to churches looking and searching and seeking, but they always come back to a person, the Way, Jesus, to find life. Always.

That is hungering and thirsting. All who lack righteousness lack God and are under the wrath of God. Anybody who dies in this world without being clothed in righteousness is hopeless and destitute. Without righteousness, we are damned and doomed. It was Blaise Pascal, the French theologian, who said about our hearts, *"We have a God-shaped vacuum."* Think about what you have been trying to fill your spiritual heart with. Do you know the difference between a Christian and a non-believer? The non-believer looks to fill their spirit, or their soul, or their heart, with something that will satisfy them and fill them up! Then they are shocked out of their minds the next day to discover they feel empty again and must continue their search. On the other hand, the Christian hungers and thirsts for more of God in their life and yet, when they are filled by Him, they *expect* to hunger and thirst the next day and know He will come and fill them again.

Ask, seek, and knock. Hunger and thirst for Him. He will rattle your bones — your dead bones. He will make you come alive.

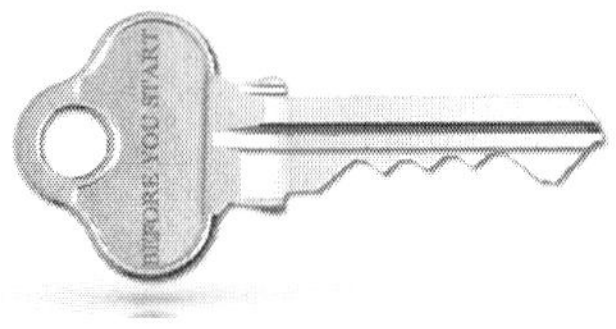

Attitude #5 • Mercy Lord!

"Blessed are the merciful, for they shall receive mercy."

-Matthew 5:7

The nearer a man gets to God, the greater he sees his sin.

-Martyn Lloyd-Jones

Let me start this chapter with some upfront statements that every believer in Christ needs to know:

- The primary emphasis of the Gospel is on being, rather than doing
- The Gospel puts a greater weight upon our attitude than on our actions
- The Gospel is about who we are and not what we do

The Sermon on the Mount involves talk about our actions, but long before the Lord Jesus gets to actions, He talks about character and disposition. Get this: A Christian is something before he/she does anything, and we must be a Christian before we can act as Christians. *Doing* is vital, but attitude is much more significant than action. Let me put it like this: We are not called to try to be Christians. This is a massive problem today in our interpretation of the Bible. It never tells us to *try* to be Christians, or to *try* to live like a Christian whenever we can. We *are* Christians and our actions are the outcome of that. Let me go one step further: we are not meant to control our Christianity. Our Christianity is meant to control us.

When we are dominated by the Truth, in Christ, then we have been made Christian by the Holy Spirit within us. The Apostle Paul tells the churches in the region of Galatia, *"I have been crucified with Christ. It is no longer I who live, but Christ who lives in me."* As a Christian, the Holy Spirit controls us at the very center of our lives, controls the very spring of our being, and He is the source of our every activity. You cannot read the Beatitudes without coming to that conclusion. The Christian life isn't polyurethane you spray on as a surface veneer. No, it's something that is happening at the very core of your being. It controls your thoughts, your outlook, your imagination, and your actions. All your activities and things to come are the result of the new nature.

And as we are confronted with the Beatitudes, we are confronted with this extraordinary portrait of what a Christian should look like. It is drawn for us, painted by the Lord Jesus. We are forced to look at ourselves, examine ourselves, and ask ourselves the question: *Am I merciful?* Well, are you? It's not a difficult thing to determine in our actions and words. The fifth Beatitude is,

> *"Blessed are the merciful, for they shall receive mercy."*　　　　　　　　　　　　　　*-Matthew 5:7*

There are two powerful parables Jesus gives us in the Gospels that we need to explore. One may be more familiar to you than the other. The first one is simply referred to as the parable of the unforgiving servant.

A king decided to clear his books and make all accounts current. There was one man who owed ten thousand talents, the Scripture says. A talent, a single talent was worth approximately twenty years' salary of a working man. Compute that and if a man lived a hundred years to work it off, it would take him two thousand lifetimes to pay his debt. Ridiculous, isn't it? You know how interest stacks up these days. Yet, the king said, *"Pay up!"* You know it's not like our modern time when, if you can't pay, they put you on a payment plan. If you default, they may seize your property, you may go bankrupt, but they don't throw you and your family into debtor's prison like they did in those ancient times. So, the man who owed ten thousand talents started doing what I would do. He started crying. He begged, 'Please, please be patient with me and I will pay it back."So, Jesus says, the King hears the man, has mercy, and forgives the debt — totally! Wipes it out! No payback at all! And you might stop and ask yourself here, *What kind of performance of crying and begging did the man put on?* But you would be wrong to concentrate on that. Rather, you need to see something about the King. You need to see his compassion, pity, and mercy for the debtor and his inability to pay him back. And it's the man's helplessness that we need to focus on.

So, the man, forgiven of his debt, goes out for a vanilla milkshake, and skips all the way down the side of the road, until he looks and sees a down-and-out man that owes him one talent. Now remember, he has just been forgiven a debt of ten thousand talents that he couldn't pay back, and this other man owes him only one talent — a measly sum. The man grabs him by the throat, and says, 'Pay me what you owe me, or I'll have you thrown in jail with all the other poor pathetic souls who can't pay their debts!"

The man begged and pleaded. He cried and said, 'Give me a little time, I promise I'll pay you back." However, the man didn't have mercy like the mercy he was shown by the king. Instead, he said no, and had the man incarcerated. A guy who knew the forgiven man, and who worked for the king, was standing on the street but a few feet away and saw everything. This incident stressed the bystander out, the Bible says, and he went and told the king what he had witnessed. You know what happens next. The royal monarch calls the man in and says, "What? Are you joking me? I forgave you of all this debt because you cried, but when this man owed you and cried for patience, but you said no, and put him in prison? Are you kidding me?" And the king reinstates the debt and throws the man in prison until he could pay it off, but you know, I know, there was no way to pay it off. It was life in prison.

Second parable. Surely you know it. A man was traveling the Jericho highway. It was a dangerous, fifteen-mile stretch of road from Jerusalem to Jericho. The man was mugged. He was beaten, robbed, and left for dead. Jesus tells us a priest walked by, then a fellow citizen soon came upon the unconscious soul. However, neither would get too close because they were religious and, if they accidently touched a dead man, then they couldn't go to temple (their place of worship) because they would have to be quarantined for a while. But then Jesus interjects someone else, and it radically changed the plot. This new character was the beaten-up man's true enemy. However, he looked and saw the beaten man and had mercy on him, picked him up, bandaged his wounds, and took care of him. Jesus asked, *"Who was the neighbor?"* And the people listening to the story said, *"The one who showed mercy."* You know the story, the Good Samaritan.

What is mercy?

First, let me tell you what mercy is not. Mercy is not looking the other way. I hope you have figured out by now that not just any religious beliefs will do. As a church leader, I can't stand by and let people do anything they want to do regarding our Lord and call it mercy. Mercy is not giving your leftover change to the Salvation Army at Christmas. Mercy is not cleaning out your closet and putting those old clothes on the front porch for the children's home truck to pick up. Mercy is not pledging to give $5 a month to the starving children's funds of the world. It's good that you think of others and want to give, but many people I have talked to have confused getting rid of old junk or a few dollars with mercy. Maybe the best way to approach mercy is to compare it to grace. When you look at these two parables of Jesus you will find several key things that we need to see in defining mercy.

Mercy is relieving the consequences of sin in the lives of others

Not only does it mean pity but, in it, a great desire to help the matter. Mercy relieves suffering in situations. In the biblical story of the *Good Samaritan* you will discover he didn't say, "I'm going to find out who did this to you and make them pay! Let's call the police!" Many people think mercy is dialing 911 when someone is in trouble. No, the Samaritan's job was to show mercy. He didn't complain about the robberies on the Jericho Road, nor did he seek to be interviewed on television about the rise in the crime rate. He sought to bring relief, period. There is a place for justice, there is a place for protest, but again, those things aren't mercy. *Mercy is getting on your hands and knees, if you have to, and doing whatever it takes to restore dignity to someone whose life has been broken by sin.*

The early church used to call Jesus The Good Samaritan. That's right, it was sort of His nickname among those early church believers. The Gospel of Matthew tells us that as Jesus healed, the religious leaders got angry and looked to kill Him, but Jesus slipped away and ordered His followers not to make Him or His whereabouts known. Then Matthew adds these words of authority to what Jesus was doing and teaching,

> *"Behold, my servant whom I have chosen,*
> *my beloved with whom my soul is well pleased.*
> *I will put my Spirit upon him,*
> *and he will proclaim justice to the Gentiles.*
> *He will not quarrel or cry aloud,*
> *nor will anyone hear his voice in the streets;*
> *a bruised reed he will not break,*
> *and a smoldering wick he will not quench,*
> *until he brings justice to victory;*
> *and in his name the Gentiles will hope."*
> *-Matthew 12:18-21*

When He encountered broken reeds, He didn't break them in half. When He met people whose lives were dimly burning flickers, He didn't blow them out. He healed them. He was drawn to them. He fanned them to flames. Jesus restored the weak and the bruised. Mercy has never been on display like it was in the life of Jesus when He walked on this planet. He never passed them by, and He never trampled them. Are you like Jesus? Do you stop like the Samaritan, or have you found a reason to pass by on the other side? Mercy relieves pain, not stirs it up and around to intensify the hurt.

Mercy doesn't hide behind unbiblical scruples to avoid help or service

You know what *"unbiblical scruples"* means don't you? It's when someone picks out of the Bible what they want to believe, and you usually become their target of action. The priest and the Levite that passed the beaten man in the ditch had things to do. If they had stopped then they would be getting away from routine, from the norm. We just want to get back to normal. According to Old Testament Law you couldn't worship if you were ceremonially unclean. What were they supposed to do? In their eyes, religion preceded mercy.

Sure, it's not a sin to be ceremonially unclean, but it is a sin to fail to show mercy. What was the problem of the priest and the Levite? They didn't want to be inconvenienced. They didn't want to give up their plans for God's plans. Yet these were the exact two things the Samaritan was ready to do. He was like Jesus. If you want to be like Jesus, then understand that opportunities to show mercy come at the worst times for your schedule. If you want to be like Jesus, then I'm not saying throw away your Daytimers, but be prepared — Jesus doesn't check your calendar before giving you an assignment.

Here's the guarantee today for your life if you pledge and commit to follow Jesus and serve Him: Your opportunity for service will inconvenience you. I know it because it happens to me constantly.

Never have I gotten bored with life and caught up with everything I need to do, and I say, *God, I need something to do...I need someone to show mercy and love...give me someone today because I have some free time from noon until 1:30.* Never. It's always the week that is falling apart in my own life that I encounter someone who needs me. It's when my car breaks down, and it's the mechanic that God wants me to share Jesus with. It's when I am at the counter and the cashier tells me it's more than I expected, and I have that look on my face of disgust, that God wants me to speak to this person about how He brings me joy. They need you. That's when God gives out tests. They're pop tests. And I don't particularly like pop tests, but they measure so much, don't they?

Too often, we think that mercy is an add-on, or something, for the big-time Christians who have more invested. We think it's for the spiritual person who has reached level ten, whatever that is. We think it's for the super-saint. Nope, it's a necessity. We need it. Living a righteous life isn't occasional, but it's habitual. Mercy is for you, and it is for you to give constantly. Our super-saintly response may be, "Well, the priest in Jesus' time and the Levite didn't know about this!" *They didn't?* It's all over the pages of the Old Testament.

For I desired **mercy***, and not sacrifice; and the knowledge of God more than burnt offerings.*
                                                        -Hosea 6:6

He has told you, O man, what is good: and what does the Lord require of you but to do justice, and to love **mercy** *and to walk humbly with your God?*
                                                        -Micah 6:8

Be merciful to me, O God, be **merciful** *to me, for in you my soul takes refuge.*   *-Psalm 57:1*

Another word for mercy is kindness. The lack of mercy is what betrays Jesus. Ask Judas. Don't forget that there is the second part of this Beatitude, and Jesus says, *"...you will obtain (receive) mercy."* You see, there's a catch.

Let's go back to that first parable of Jesus we were talking about earlier — the king, and the man whom the king forgave and then repealed the gift. Does this mean that God only forgives when I forgive those who have done me wrong? No, and understand two things, if that were so then nobody is going to be forgiven nor will they see heaven. Another thing is, if that is true then we must cancel out the whole doctrine and idea of grace.

Here's an inside secret: Scripture interprets Scripture. It's a necessity to consider the whole counsel of God when interpreting Scripture. Paul tells Timothy in 2 Timothy 2, that he must study the Scripture and, *rightly divide the Word of truth.* It means to interpret it with integrity and handle it correctly. The parable means that I am only truly forgiven when I am truly repentant. True repentance means you understand you have no other way out of this world but by God, and by His mercy and grace alone. So when I realize this, and understand this by grasping it in faith, then I understand I am required to forgive others. You can't fake your salvation. If that is what you are doing, quit! You can put on a false front for a while, maybe for years, but the Holy Spirit will find you out. The monks of old would hide out in isolation from the rest of the world thinking it would put them on a fast track to God. It doesn't and never will. Obedience to Him every day is what He demands.

This is huge: You should continue to see how the Beatitudes go in order. You must start with *poor in spirit,* meaning you have no righteousness in and of yourself. It comes from God. Then mourn your lack of righteousness, that's sin. And afterwards you look in the mirror and take right inventory and see that you have nothing to give to Him. There is no way to rescue yourself. You have no goodness hidden down deep, so then you will seek your meekness. No one can say anything bad about you when you are true to yourself and see that you are truly lost without Him. No one can say anything that is going to hurt your feelings when you understand the worst about yourself. When you see Jesus, you hunger and thirst for His goodness, His righteousness.

After you are poor in spirit, mourn, are meek, and hunger for rightness, then your attitude towards everyone will be completely and entirely changed. I am truly forgiven when I am truly repentant. When you receive His mercy, then you can look at others with a Christian eye of mercy for them. Get this: when you really experience His mercy and His grace (His gift to you), and know you are not going to be allowed into His presence without His mercy then, and only then, are you able to see with spiritual eyes this world and the dupes of the enemy. His goal is to pull the wool over your eyes. And it is only when you really see others who do you wrong, after you have been freely showered with His mercy, that you are able to look at people who are mean, conniving, and wicked, and have pity on them.

The Bible describes those without Christ as the wicked. They are deep into serving the enemy and they don't even know it. They are wicked because of sin. They are enslaved to Satan. Understand that you would be, too, yet for the grace and mercy of God. It is when we comprehend it, and live it, that we will have mercy. As a Christian, whenever you see anyone in a state of sin, your reaction is to be one of pity. It's sad that they are in the grips of darkness. We must confront them with the love and truth of Jesus.

A popular response is the phrase, *God hates sin, but loves the sinner.* Sort of, but I wouldn't go there. God hates the sin in the sinner, therefore God hates the sinner. The Bible says it! However, the Good News of the Gospel is that even though God hates the sin, He has mercy for the sinner. And when the sinner turns to Him there is forgiveness, and we are cleansed of it.

Stephen, the man of God in Acts 7, was preaching his heart out in front of sinners and people who despised him. They hated his guts. Yet, he never trod lightly to avoid hurting their feelings. His message was the truth about sin. He preached about the effects of the enemy and the result of sin. The religious people of the day scorned him. As he wrapped up his famous sermon, they picked up rocks and pelted him to death. Scripture says as he gasped some of his last breaths he said, "God, don't hold this against them." That's mercy. When you truly realize the mercy God has shown you, then you can't help showing it around town to co-workers, friends, and family. You appreciate that if it were not for mercy you, too, would be unknowing about God and stuck in sin.

Now, look at Him on the Cross. The Lord Jesus never sinned. He never did any harm to anyone. He came and preached the truth. He came to seek and save that which was lost. Imagine it. Look at Him… there He is… nailed to the Cross, suffering in agony for your sin. Does He look around and grit His teeth and say, "I hope you all rot in hell." No, He said, *"Father, forgive them."* Why? They didn't know what they were doing. They are victims, they are governed and dominated by sin. He had mercy. My friends, we are to become like that.

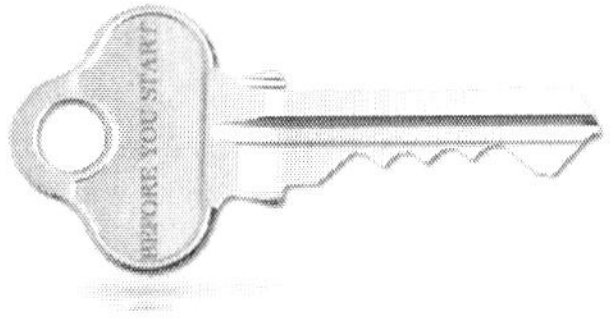

Attitude #6 • Purity

"Blessed are the pure in heart, for they shall see God."

-Matthew 5:8

Our calling isn't to follow our hearts. Our calling is to have our hearts informed and directed by the clear and plain teaching of the Word of God.   -RC Sproul

Not too long ago I was reading and studying Psalm 69 where David, the Psalmist, begins with, 'Save me, God!" Believe it or not, that's a good way to start your prayers. It's maturity and strength in believing God will rescue you from your troubles and current bad situation. David continues and cries out, "The water is up to my neck! I am sinking in quicksand." You get the picture, don't you? The pressure is high, the intensity is at the boiling point, and he's drowning. He continues, "I'm weary, my throat is parched, my vision is dimming, and I just wait for you God."

I put down my Bible and I thought, "I've had a comfortable week. I'm not living in a hamlet on the front lines of Ukraine as the Russians invade. I'm not living on the Straits of Taiwan as China dangles the carrot of annexation in front of me. I'm not poor and destitute

59

begging on the streets of New Delhi. I'm not homeless and country-less, trying to cross a border to escape my captors. As a matter of fact, I've had plenty to eat today. I slept eight hours last night. I went to a ballgame with a friend. I played a relaxing round of golf. I ate dinner with my wife. I talked to my son, I talked to my parents, I talked to my in-laws. I laughed with my buddies. I ate apple pie! I'm not up to my neck or sinking in mud! My vision is good. My throat is fine. This isn't talking to me or about me." Or is it?

You should realize something from this massive Psalm: your problem is not the stuff on the outside, and real joy doesn't come from the external. The issue and the whole deal every day, in every way, is the heart. We avoid the issues of the heart by masking our outward appearance. If we decorate the exterior, we think, then no one will ever find out about our interior. It's eight verses in, but Jesus gets right to the heart, your heart.

He says, *"Blessed are the pure in heart,"* that is what Christianity is all about. The Gospel of Jesus Christ is concerned with the heart. The emphasis is on the heart. Read and study the accounts of Jesus and His teaching in the New Testament and you will find that the whole time He is talking about the heart. The same is true about the Old Testament. Let me emphasize in bold type so you don't forget this chapter, **it's about the heart... my heart, your heart**. Jesus puts the emphasis on the nucleus of our lives because the religious structure of that time, the Pharisees, concentrated on the appearance of things, while ignoring the inner being. You know by now we are not talking about religion in this book. If you want to see what religion looks like, then look no further than the Pharisees because they personified it. Religion is what you look like to everyone else. But it's the heart that matters to God, and the heart is the whole teaching of Jesus.

Here's another place where I place an emphasis: **Doctrine**. It's massive! It's huge that we understand, and teach and live, the precise Word of God. What is doctrine? It's the holy text. It's what God says and what it means. And a quick little timeout: You cannot make the Word of God mean what you want it to mean. Be very careful and wary of those who say, "This is the way I interpret the Bible." There is only one way to interpret the text. It's not what you believe it says and what I believe it says and we will agree to disagree. No, it's what God says, and what He means. Doctrine is important. Now, we can go back to the regularly scheduled chapter of this book.

Intellect is important. Intellectual comprehension of the Gospel and what it means is big and essential, and understanding it is vital. I know a lot of people who are well-versed in Bible knowledge and church stuff. I've encountered many who have read the Bible over and over. I also know people who can quote Scripture, but it's not just a matter of doctrine and the mind. Jesus puts the emphasis on the heart. The Pharisees were always ready to reduce the way of life and living to a moral conduct, good ethics, or a manner of behavior. *But the heart of the matter is the matter of the heart!*

What do I mean when I say heart? According to Scriptural usage, it is the center of your personality. It's not just your emotions, and not just your affections. It's the total man, the total woman. God is speaking of your mind, your will, and your heart. Do you get it? It's *"Blessed are the pure in heart,"* and not just the surface stuff. It's not just the outside, but it's living for God in a relationship with Jesus Christ, and that is heart-deep. With our Lord, it always starts with the heart. However...

The Heart Is always the center of your Troubles

Have you overlooked that it was in Paradise that Adam and Eve fell? Modern man is always looking for bliss and some sort of Nirvana (Buddhist false teaching of a heavenly state of being). The Garden of Eden was a perfect environment where we all went wrong. Having the perfect place to live, with all the money, and with all the friends, doesn't mean a perfect life as you well know.

In Exodus 23, there is a fantastic appearance of God. It's a dramatic scene. A picture unfolds that most have never paid much attention to. Moses is with Aaron, Hur, Nadab, Abihu, and the seventy elders of Israel. Here's the panoramic view: It's the Ten Commandments scene, where God has just given them the Law by which they are to live. And chapter 24 is the confirmation, or the ratification, of the Covenant. There was a sacrifice and the people said in unison, *"We will obey God!"* And Moses takes the blood of the sacrifice and throws it on the people. Now probably not everyone would have been hit with the blood, but it's a symbolic signal of commitment. God then calls out Moses, Aaron, Nadab, and Hur and the seventy. Look at this:

> *Then they climbed the mountain—Moses and Aaron, Nadab and Abihu, and seventy of the elders of Israel—and saw the God of Israel. He was standing on a pavement of something like sapphires—pure, clear sky-blue. He didn't hurt these pillar-leaders of the Israelites: They saw God; and they ate and drank.*   *-Exodus 24:9-11*

What? What in the world! Are you paying attention to this? They *saw* God! What was the appearance of God like? Dear Reader, let me be right up front with you here: This is why I am a Christ-follower — because one day I will see Him. Not only will I see Him, but I will see Him every day! I will live with Him, and so will you if you have humbled your heart and turned from sin.

Sapphire pavement will be baby stuff compared to what we are going to walk on in that day. However, we are presented with this Beatitude concerning the heart, and with this account in Exodus of seeing God. What does that mean? Does it really mean that this is objective and visible or is it spiritual? It's a great question, but a complicated answer, and ultimately cannot be answered. But look at the evidence of appearances of God. Later, Moses sees God's glory in Exodus 33. Moses asks to see God and God says, "Moses, you can't look at ME and live! I'm holy." So, God hides Moses in a cleft of a rock and passes by so that Moses can look at Him from behind. This is not the only sighting of God in the Bible. There are other theophanies in

Scripture that suggest that you can't just look upon God with the naked eye. Then there is the statement by our Lord Himself:

> *"And the Father who sent me has himself borne witness about me. His voice you have never heard, his form you have never seen...."*   *-John 5:37*

> *"Everyone who has heard and learned from the Father comes to me— not that anyone has seen the Father except he who is from God; he has seen the Father."*   *-John 6:45-46*

> *No one has ever seen God; if we love one another, God abides in us and his love is perfected in us.*
> *-1 John 4:12*

> *"Whoever has seen me has seen the Father."*
> *-John 14:9*

This is what Scripture says about what God looks like, about seeing Him. Is God transcendent or imminent? Both. Why can't we see God? Have you ever thought about that? Because of His glory! Because of His purity. It is because of His holiness. If He is like us, then why do we want to look at Him or see Him? All we know is this promise from Jesus, that those who are pure in heart will see Him. The Christian is very well-versed in seeing God. We see Him in His wonderful and tremendous creation. We see Him in the scenic nature. We see Him in the dramatic and benign events of history. The Christian knows He is near. The Christian has a certain knowledge, maybe instinct or feeling, and enjoys His presence. In Hebrews 11, a famous chapter of faith, it gives us more insight into the vision of Moses and him seeing God,

> *By faith Moses, when he was born, was hidden for three months by his parents, because they saw that the child was beautiful, and they were not afraid of the king's edict. By faith Moses, when he was grown up, refused to be called the son of Pharaoh's daughter, choosing rather to be mistreated with*

Full disclosure: I haven't seen Him but, like Moses, there have been several times in my life where I have looked back, and I've seen His footprints. My response is to say, "Ohhhh, okay, now I see Him." It's those many times — I have gone through it, and you have gone through it too. It's the junk, the bad stuff, maybe even the existential hell of life itself, and you are up to your neck in it. It is when you are sinking in it, and you cry to Him, "God, save me, please rescue me,"and it's then that we realize, it's the condition of our heart that matters. He will allow bad things to happen, He will even allow sickness leading up to death for His purpose in your life. He will go to the extremes for you to see Him and trust Him so you can live a right life in front of Him. It's a heart issue.

I know there are the humanists who say, "No, it's about politics. No, it's about the financial state of our country. No, it's about solving communism, socialism, fascism, or racism." We will cry about our rights and our freedoms to do whatever we want. And in this progressive age we imagine that it's about homosexual rights, transgender privileges, or body mutilation choices. In reality, our exclamation is, "It's about me and everything I want to do to make myself happy!" No, my friend, it's all about the condition of your heart.

God invites Moses and the leadership of Israel to a party in Exodus 24. It is quite remarkable to read about the décor and ponder the happenings of this oft forgotten scene. There is a sapphire parquet floor! To even consider the sparkling, ostentatiously eloquent scene is fascinating. After the party, God tells Moses to come and receive the Ten Commandments...

Wait! What? Does it really say that certain people were selected to have dinner with God, on blue jeweled floors? Michelin star restaurants today couldn't or wouldn't dare compete. Don't you think there were cheers and toasts with bursts of joyous and festive yells of victory? Did Moses and the seventy have the feeling that they had arrived? Were they thinking, *this is what it's all about. This is what makes it all worthwhile. We made it!* Hold on — I'm getting to the point.

Moses and Joshua were going to be gone for a few hours, maybe a few days, and Moses found it necessary to have a judge to settle disputes. Disputes? They just had an elaborate dinner with the Creator of the Universe, down with priceless decorations! If that doesn't tell you it's always a matter of the heart, then nothing does. And on a mountainside a few thousand years later, the Lord Jesus tells us that if you want to be blessed, then blessed are those who are pure in heart. So, maybe now is the time you need to put an end to your prayers to God, *bless me God, bless me, give me more and more stuff!*

What blessings do we really need? Here's what *Blessed are the pure in heart* is truly about: He has already blessed us more than we can handle. Realize and understand the blessing of the Lord Jesus dying for you, being buried, and raised again. All the while during the Passion,

He suffered and bled so that we can look forward with great hope of His second coming and His appearance. It will be dazzling!

You cannot make yourself a Christian. The proposal of the Gospel is that He lifts us up out of the pit of life, out of the hell of life, to raise us up into the heavens with Him. It's a supernatural thing. And here again in the Beatitudes we are faced with an attitude we must have, and it's progressing to the point where we learn the only way to have a pure heart is to start at the point where we understand we have impure hearts. A fantastic mark of Christian maturity is recognizing your sinful self.

The Greek word for pure translates to *clean*. Another word to describe it is *single*. Being single-hearted instead of double-minded. One of the best definitions of a pure heart comes from Psalm 86.

> *Teach me your way, O Lord, that I may walk in*
> *your truth; unite my heart to fear your name.*
> *-Psalm 86:11*

Our trouble starts with a divided heart. Why would God reveal Himself in His glory to someone who has an impure heart? We have this heart that wants to know Him some of the time but wants to do what we want to do the rest of the time. He knows this and He calls us to have a pure heart. We need to seek to have a pure heart. That is why the Psalmist begs God to unite our heart. A united heart is a single-minded heart, and a pure heart.

We know that a house divided doesn't stand. Marriages and families are constantly under attack from the enemy. Satan wants to separate truth from the heart to cause friction and, ultimately, detachment. There are three aspects to the heart:

- Wholeness
- Cleanliness
- Desirous

Pure in heart means to be like the Lord Himself, *who did no sin, nor was guile found in Him.* A united heart is one that seeks to desire Him, meaning to desire God. The result is the desire to love Him, and to serve Him. It's not *you have to*, or even *you want to*, but *you get to* worship Him. Jesus says to us, only those who have that attitude will see Him. Interestingly, just a decade or two ago the modern day churched praised the advances in technology that we use in church. However, in just a few short years, it's the cause of people staying home. They say that they can just "watch church" on television.

People haven't stopped coming to church because it's not cool in their lives anymore. They haven't stopped reading the Bible because they don't understand it, and they haven't rejected Jesus because they don't feel it. They've done it because they understand well that our God demands purity. And the human soul living in a natural world doesn't want purity. So, many have created their own idol: themselves. The most serious statement I can make is that you will not see God — it doesn't matter how passionate you are about church, worship or spiritual gifts — you will not see Him without a pure heart. Your praise and lifting your hands will not take the place of righteous living. You must see that the whole of Christianity is to bring us to seeing God. How can I make my heart pure? You must allow Him to cleanse you. You can't do it yourself. The book of James says,

> **Draw near to God**, and he will **draw near** to you. Cleanse your hands, you sinners, and purify your hearts, you double-minded.   *-James 4:8*

The Apostle Paul tells the church at Philippi and Rome,

> *...for it is God who works in you, both to will and to work for his good pleasure.*
>   *-Philippians 2:13*

> *For if you live according to the flesh you will die, but if by the Spirit you put to death the deeds of the body, you will live.*   *-Romans 8:13*

If I understand this right, everyone will meet God. But hold on! Yes, you will meet Him at the Great Judgement seat — but not everyone will see Him. Seeing Him is reserved for those who have a pure heart. I am going to see God. I've never had a sit-down with a President, and I've never met a world leader. I don't live next door to a professional athlete, and I don't hang out with television stars. I think of Abraham, Isaac, Jacob, Joseph, Moses, David, John the Baptist, and Paul, who will all be in glory, but they don't stack up to our King. Our King, our Savior, the Lord Jesus, has promised me that I will see Him.

As I get older, my eyesight is fading more each year. I need to see my Optometrist annually, and each year my vision is a tiny bit worse. So, I get new contacts and a new pair of glasses to keep reading and driving. But one day, even if these old eyes of mine go completely black, the beautiful promise that I am looking forward to is to look at Him.

I love the movie, *Rudy*, the true story about the 1970's runt player for the fighting Irish of Notre Dame. Daniel "Rudy" Ruettiger was on the scout team, but in the last game of his final year, he got to dress out with the team and take the field. It's one of those inspiring movies that make you want to cheer and cry all at the same time. In one of the last scenes of the movie as Rudy's dad goes to "the house that Rockne built," for the very first time in his life, he gazes around at the loud crowd of Notre Dame stadium before the start of the game and says, "This is the most beautiful sight these eyes have ever seen." I cry every time I watch that scene because Ned Beatty says it with such feeling and pathos. I imagine one day, in a much different and greater scene, finally realizing the race I have run with anticipation for Him and Him alone, my once fading eyes will see clearly and I will gaze into His eyes, simply because He allows me to. And my eyes will not be able to contain the love, the feeling, the truth of the moment, and it will be all those things forever. Paul says,

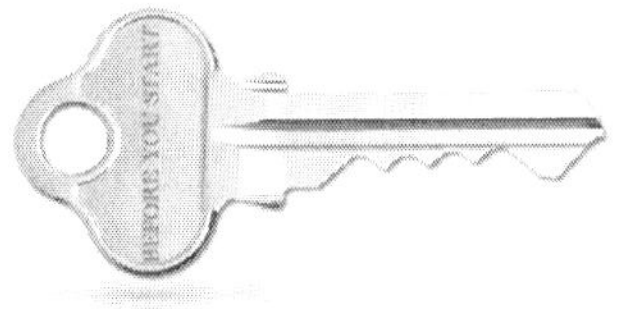

Attitude #7 • All We are saying...

"Blessed are the peacemakers, for they shall be called sons of God."
-Matthew 5:9

Habakkuk looked to God and ceased to look at his difficulty. That is the true basis of spiritual peace.   -Martyn Lloyd-Jones

The Internet and social media allow us to travel the world without ever having to leave our homes. I have a friend on one social media platform who lives in Scotland. We've never met, but I suppose he's a little more than a friend. Rather, he's a long-lost kinsman. His last name Is Dowey. We've never talked on the phone nor met in person One day last year, for some reason unknown to me, he left for Kyiv — that's right, Ukraine. In this decade, Ukraine is a war-torn place. I kept up with his travels while he posted pictures of himself with battle-shaken people that he met walking the streets and hiding from the Russian army. He linked videos from a hotel room of the bombing of this Slavic country.

Again, I don't know what he was trying to prove, yet he was interviewed on a European news channel about his encounters and sights. Mesmerized and watching the video, one can see the weariness on his face and hear it in his voice as he talks about the Russians closing in on the capitol. He talked about the terrifying sounds and images. He's a brave man, I suppose. He doesn't fear the Russians! More frightening than that, he has no fear of God.

His social media profile says that he doesn't believe in God. From the pictures, it looks like my Dowey relative is approximately sixty-five years old. His profile declares his atheism since he was five years old, and he still doesn't believe in the Almighty today. It's heartbreaking, and as I thought about our God, His holiness, His majesty, my mind went to Psalm 78. The Psalmist, Asaph, talks about the people after God had rescued them from captivity and Moses had led them out of Egypt. Naturally, we think that when God rescues us, we shape up and try to fly straight, but we don't. And they didn't either. Asaph writes that they sinned even more. They rebelled and tested God by making demands on Him. They provoked Him, and sadly, they grieved Him. However, don't think for a moment that God says, *It's okay, I'll deal with it in my own way internally. Don't worry about my feelings, I'll get over it.* Not a chance. Psalms records this about our God:

Therefore, when the Lord heard, he was full of wrath; a fire was kindled against Jacob; his anger rose against Israel, because they did not believe in God and did not trust his saving power.
-Psalm 78:21-22

Subsequently, the writer further states that when the people had trouble and started dying, they changed their tune again and began flattering God with their words. But in their hearts, they were flippant, not meaning what they were saying. They lied to God. Nor were they faithful. Yet God kept loving them, and loving them more, and ministering to them by giving His grace and mercy.

I started thinking about this Dowey kinsman over in Ukraine staring at the enemy army as they were creeping toward him with all their might. The news media reported that Soviet-era tanks formed a line in unison for forty miles. Search for the photos yourself, in the online news, and look at the intimidating pictures of cruel humanity. Everybody knows Vladimir Putin, Russia's long-time leader, is armed with nuclear weapons. If my distant cousin who doesn't know God in a relationship with the Lord Jesus, and if the terror and visuals of war, don't make you begin to contemplate the claims of Christ, then what will? Are atheists really living in foxholes in the Ukraine? It only led me to think even more: If he hasn't seen terror or dread or felt trepidation and trembling by now, oh the horror he faces when he looks upon the face of the Holy God! My dear kinsman, you desperately need Jesus — you desperately need to know the fear of God.

Nothing tests us, examines us, or humbles us like the Beatitudes. Nothing! *"Blessed are the peacemakers"* speaks to you and me in a unique way. There is nothing more fatal in this world than thinking you can live the goodness of the Beatitudes, yet not be a Christ-follower or desire to be one. However, this modern-day culture tries to do it repeatedly and habitually. It takes a new person to live the Jesus lifestyle. If you are not a new person in Christ, if He has not refreshed you for fresh living, then it's crucial you grasp this Beatitude so you can grow more in Christ.

Peace is usually that thing we don't think about until there is war or turmoil in our lives. Peace is on the back burner of our minds until we are desperate for it. It is often a superficial cry or a symbolic gesture we make when we are clueless what to say or do. Peace to most people means just getting along and mouthing, *I love you.* In case you don't know it yet, NATO isn't working to bring world peace. The United Nations isn't working to bring stability. Have you ever seen a UN Peacekeeper? They may call them peacekeepers, but they wear bullet-proof vests and helmets, carry machine guns, and pack grenades on their belts. Peace settlements and peace agreements have been drawn up and signed for thousands of years. If they worked, then we would have peace already. The truth is, most people have no clue what peace is, nor how to get it. Do you know you can go to www.peacemaker.un.com and click on any country and find the peace agreements that have been made throughout history? Peace *agreements*. Plural. How many do you need until you have peace? It's like getting to the center of a Tootsie Pop — you just need to keep licking!

When Jesus makes this statement, *"blessed are the peacemakers,"* the Jews in the audience scoffed. They shook their heads. They had that puzzled look of disgust on their faces. They had assumed the kingdom of God would be ushered in with some tremendous military campaign. They envisioned the Messiah riding in on a white horse, wielding a silver sword. They dreamed of getting revenge on the Romans and the rest of the world by having their Savior come and defeat the army of Rome and other enemies of God. The religious people had warped the kingdom into something materialistic in nature. And even in these days, people still want to monetize the kingdom of God.

The common belief was that He was going to come and be another great king, but this time would exact absolute vengeance. Even John the Baptist seems to think this to a certain degree. Remember, when he sent two of his disciples with that famous question to the Lord, *Are you the* **ONE** *or should we look for another?* Recall when Jesus fed the five thousand and they tried to take HIM by force and push Him to be king? Jesus said, *"You don't understand, my kingdom is not of this world."* And here we learn something about this king, He says, *"Blessed are the peacemakers."*

What fantastic timing for our world. This world longs to know the meaning of this Beatitude. Give prudence here and listen to this caveat. For two thousand years, and especially with the religious, progressive, social gospel, woke movement in the last several years, there has been this movement to adopt and accept and live the Beatitudes, but to forget the rest of the Bible, including the rest of the New Testament. Here's the caution: you can't live this Beatitude, or any of the others, without allowing the Holy Spirit to indwell your life in the person of Jesus Christ.

Jesus says, *"Blessed are the peacemakers."* So, why are peacemakers blessed? Because they are so unlike everyone else. I don't think you have a right to stand up and demand peace in Canada, peace in Ukraine, peace in Chicago, peace in Hong Kong, or flash that universal peace sign with your fingers or march for peace, unless you know what peace really is. Jesus is talking about something far more important than a treaty between nations and tribes here. He is talking about peace with God.

We want to know why there are wars in this world and when the myriad, endless international conflicts will end. Exactly what is the tension between nations? We wonder where WWIII will begin. Why is there fighting on some street at this very moment? We question why there is such high divorce rate, who is responsible for murder being up, and when racism will end. We worry about the increase in home invasions, and consider the presence of so much unhappiness, turmoil, and discord. What's wrong with this world? Only one answer — sin. Nothing else explains it better — just sin. You cannot begin to understand the problems of this world until you accept the New Testament doctrine regarding man and sin. If you don't then you will just look to sign worthless, meaningless stacks of paper while calling it peace. Again, these types of people have no idea of what God is talking about.

The world is blind to the things of God. The world rejects God's peace. The trouble, according to Scripture, is the heart. Until the heart is changed you will never have true peace in your life. You will never understand all the whys and hows in all your questions. If the trouble is in the fountain, quit pouring all your money and efforts downstream. Go to the source. Too often the church has been preaching the wrong thing. We teach and preach human efforts instead of praying and seeking His answer. Out of an old heart is going to come what you've always had in it: staleness. You can't patch up an old heart to have a new attitude. What Jesus continuously teaches us from His Holy Word is that you need a *new* heart to live a *new* life in Christ.

> *And he called the people to him and said to them, "Hear and understand: it is not what goes into the mouth that defiles a person, but what comes out of the mouth; this defiles a person." Then the disciples came and said to him, "Do you know that the Pharisees were offended when they heard this saying?" He answered, "Every plant that my heavenly Father has not planted will be rooted up. Let them alone; they are blind guides. And if the blind lead the blind, both will fall into a pit." But Peter said to him, "Explain the parable to us." And he said, "Are you also still without understanding? Do you not see that whatever goes into the mouth passes into the stomach and is expelled? But what comes out of the mouth proceeds from the heart, and this defiles a person. For out of the heart come evil thoughts, murder, adultery, sexual immorality, theft, false witness, slander."*
>
> *-Matthew 15:10-19*

If you are going to be a peacemaker, and if you want peace in your life, you need a new heart. *What is a peacemaker?* It's not an easy-going person, and it's not simply a certain look on your face. Why are so many of today's Christians out there with solemn looks on their faces? Where's the joy these days from following Christ? A peacemaker is not someone who avoids trouble, or someone who looks to appease others. Avoiding war doesn't make you a peacemaker. *A true peacemaker is the one who desires peace!* That is first and foremost with God and in God. Peace from what with God?

Some of the churches today really get it, and they are walking and praying and seeking God. They are good at presenting the Gospel of Jesus Christ. Gospel simply means "good news." The good news is that we are sinners, and that God sent His only Son to rescue you and me by dying on a Cross. He was buried and He rose again so that you too, by transferring your sins to the Cross of Christ, will be rescued. You too will be saved. You too, in this spiritual body you live in, will join Him in eternity. That's the Good News. Here's what we are not good at in the modern church: sharing the bad news. If you have good news, then you must also have bad news.

My routine every morning is real and rather symbolic to me. I start my day by quickly scrambling myself some eggs (they are so good, too!). I grab my dark espresso coffee, and head to my study. While I am scarfing down my breakfast, I peruse the news, and then the local obituaries. I always begin the day with bad news. Show me the bad news first because then, for the rest of the day, I am seeking the Good News. Serving Him by walking with Him is the good news I crave. Get the bad news out of the way, I say. It is essential to know the bad news before you come to Christ. If you don't know the bad news, then how does the good news make sense? Do you know the bad news for those outside of Christ? Read Psalm 78.

> *He let loose on them his burning anger, wrath, indignation, and distress, a company of destroying angels. He made a path for his anger; he did not spare them from death, but gave their lives over to the plague.*　　　　　*-Psalm 78:49-50*

He let loose. The bad news is that God is upset. And upset doesn't begin to describe the anger of God. Whose idea was it to shape our Omnipotent, Omniscient God into a pipsqueak? Where did the idea originate to perpetually paint a picture of our God as a god that puts up with anything? Why do we think He is satisfied with a wimpy, *I'm sorry* from us, thirty seconds before taking our last breath? Do we really believe He is going to say, "Okay," and wipe the slate clean? Are you joking? Who told you God loves you unconditionally, and why did you believe it? There are conditions! You give Him your life when you commit to following Him.

We continue to believe there is absolutely no difference between the righteous and the ones who cuss Him to His face, while making up excuses not to be involved with the Bride of Christ (the local church). Yet many give repetitive justifications not to serve the Bride, and present flimsy excuses not to give at all to God's work, all the while thinking everything is cool with them and God because they sport a cross around their neck. Look again at what the Psalmist (Psalm 78) said. *He let loose*, and it seemed like He was holding it back. *He let loose* on them His burning anger, wrath, indignation, and distress.

And here's the bad news: without Christ in your life, there is no peace with God. No peace whatsoever. Your soul is wandering and scavenging the allies of life looking to fit in somewhere, anywhere. Your heart is empty even though you've spent your life's savings on trying to fill it and can't figure out why it's not full to capacity. Your spirit is homeless, meaningless, and you feel hopeless. There is no peace without God in a relationship with Christ Jesus.

If you are at peace with God, then here's what it looks like:

New View of You

Remember the first Beatitude. Poor in Spirit. The Christian has come to see themselves as having nothing to offer to God, nothing to give, and empty before Him. Do you want a great test of whether you are a Christ-follower? Buckle up because you're probably not ready for this answer. Jesus said, *"He that loves his life will lose it."* He is talking about your old life. He is talking about what the Bible refers to as the natural man, the way you were born — that person. It is that person without Christ. And then there is that seemingly outlandish verse from Luke 24, from our Lord that describes true devotedness to Him:

> *"If anyone comes to me and does not hate his own father and mother and wife and children and brothers and sisters, yes, and even his own life, he cannot be my disciple."* -Luke 24:26

You may as well let me go ahead and state it. Jesus wants you to hate that person, or else you can't love Him. A new view of you involves prioritizing God in your life. If He is not first, then you cannot understand love.

Two now In You

When you come to Christ you get a new heart. It is the heart of Christ living in you (in the person of the Holy Spirit) and you in Him. In the book of Romans, Paul calls that old self the *old man*. When your old man wants to go back to *normal*, your answer is, *leave me alone! I don't live there anymore! I now live for Christ and with Christ.* Then why doesn't God just take the old heart away? He does. It's called heaven. But here's how to look at it — you now know the truth. You see how and why others act like hell and are pawns of Satan. Your response isn't to dismiss them, but to understand and pray for them and have mercy and grace for when they do you wrong. That new heart in Christ now gives you an entirely new perspective of life! Now you see that treaties don't work. Peace is from Him.

World gives you up

You don't give up sin, sin gives you up. Draw close to God and He will draw close to you, then sin and the world will leave you alone. The peacemaker has one goal — to glorify God in his/her life. That's it. God made man perfect, and the world was meant to be Paradise. When there is quarreling and strife, international disputes, and war, it detracts from God's glory. When God's people practice malice and revenge, they are far from the works God has for them. Face it, the world doesn't like true peacemakers, it's wants hellraisers! God came for us to have and know peace. How do I live it out?

Zip It!

Morton Downey Jr. had this late-night talk show back in the Eighties. He was this ultra-conservative pundit that loved to argue with people with left-leaning political and social views. On his television show, he would get in these folks' faces and yell, "Zip it!" It was his way to tell them to shut up.

> *Know this, my beloved brothers: let every person be quick to hear, slow to speak, slow to anger.*
> *-James 1:19*

The very best way to be a peacemaker is to be slow to talk. Let me tell you something else — don't repeat something when you know it's going to bring harm. I'm talking about opinions people have about others. We must control our tongues as Christians. Stop repeating unkind things. Your lame excuse is *well, that's just the way I am, I have to get it out there, I have to be able to express myself."* Then, please let me express myself, *You're not a Christian.* How does that sound? Not too good. The very first thing you must know after God has bestowed His peace on you is that you are to be a peacemaker, and that starts with zipping it!

Think before you speak

Ask yourself questions: What are the implications? How does this reflect on the church? How does what I am about to say reflect on my Savior? We are the bride of Christ!

I did a wedding recently for a friend, and as the bride came down the aisle, someone said, "Those shoes don't match." I heard someone else say, "Who's she kidding? She's been married four times!" Someone else yelled out, "I know her, she shouldn't be wearing white if you know what I mean!" I'm joking, that didn't happen. But I've heard such things so many times in the church, and the church is the bride of Christ. Quit running others down and questioning their salvation by spreading lies and rumors.

Speak Loudly

Whoa! You just said... that was about... yeah, that was about your mouth, and your old natural way, and shutting it down. But if you are going to be a peacemaker — if Christians are all called to be peacemakers — then we should work to bring others into the fellowship of peace. We must approach the people in our communities and invite them to come to Christ. We must meet them where they are, we must invite them, and we must speak up, to see them turn to God in a relationship with Christ Jesus.

Peace sign Christian

The problem of warring between friends, family, and churches in this world is fake Christians. Just flashing the Christian sign by coming to church isn't going to change anyone. Adopting the Christian language of *Amen* and *Hallelujah* is not going to bring peace either. You must live it. God demands peace in the Bride. I have seen more fights in church than I care to remember. I have some fantastically entertaining stories that I will save for another book. But take my word for it, those factions and protests in the pews were nasty. As the pastor of my church, and with my fellow Elders, we will not put up with it. We will not put up with bad attitudes. My goodness, this book is on the Be-attitudes! Be peaceful!

> *'Blessed are the peacemakers, for they shall be called sons of God."*　　　　　*-Matthew 5:9*

The word *called* means to be owned. We are owned by God. If a peacemaker is a child of God, then he is like His Father.

> *Now may the God of peace who brought again from the dead our Lord Jesus....*
> 　　　　　*-Hebrews 13:20*

The Son of God came into this world because of sin. Sin brings war, discord, chaos, mayhem, commotion, turbulence, and pain. God comes to bring peace to your life amidst it all. He has come. He has done something about it. He has laid down His life. He has humbled Himself on the Cross. He died. He was buried. He rose again. Those early Christians had to learn it too. They wanted the easy way out and wanted God to squash the enemy in the war. The Lord Jesus brought a war they could neither fathom nor fight. He fought sin with His blood, and peace flows forward. Our God reminds us that it's a matter of the heart. He is the peacemaker. And He sent the Prince of Peace to make it right.

> *And he is the head of the body, the church. He is the beginning, the firstborn from the dead, that in everything he might be preeminent. For in him all the fullness of God was pleased to dwell, and through him to reconcile to himself all things, whether on earth or in heaven, making peace by the blood of his cross.* *-Colossians 1:18-20*

The Cross of Jesus Christ wasn't symbolic of war with this world and the king of this world, Satan, it is war! God knew it was going to be a blood bath. The blood of the Savior smeared over the ground where He bled and died. It was a bloodbath — a blood bath — so that He could bathe you in His love. It was a blood bath to rescue you from His anger, His wrath, and His indignation. This shows us Our God, even though He is upset, is the PEACEMAKER! Make peace with Him today, don't wait until it's too late.

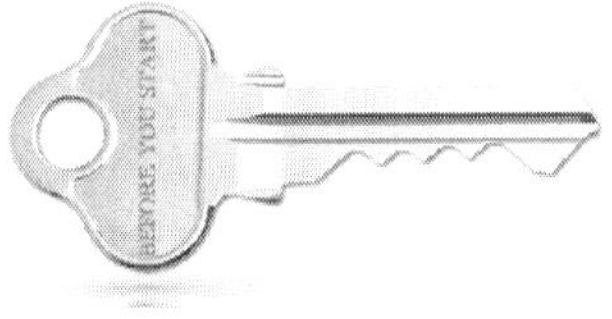

Attitude #8 • New Religion

"Blessed are those who are persecuted for righteousness' sake, for theirs is the kingdom of heaven.

"Blessed are you when others revile you and persecute you and utter all kinds of evil against you falsely on my account. <u>Rejoice and be glad</u>, for your reward is great in heaven, for so they persecuted the prophets who were before you." -Matthew 5:10-12

Whatever God takes, be still thankful for what He leaves.

-John Flavel

Let's just say I'm starting a new religion (don't worry I'm not, I want to make a point). If I were going to start a new religion today, I know exactly where to start. I know exactly where I can find a few thousand people and I know, I know, I know they would give to it and support it, and attend. I even have a name for my new religion. I call it *V-L*. That's short for Virtuous Living. We live in a society that sports a new conviction, and new chapters are popping up all the time. Virtuous living is an ethical lifestyle. It's one of keeping a self-defined code of morals that one may think is upright. Virtuous living makes us feel good about ourselves. *Yes, I'll pay a few more dollars for a gallon of gas, if it* *means those folks in the Ukraine can have peace one day.* Virtuous living is *yeah, I'll do this church thing if it makes them feel better, or makes me feel better about myself.*

Some call it mini-martyrdom. *Hey, look at me, I've got a LGBTQ+ flag on my bumper sticker.* You're checking out, and the person at the cash register says, "would you like to give to the children's home today?" And you look around as the other people in line stare at you demanding you hurry, and you say as you force a little smile, "Of course, anything for the children!" It's V-L. It is the religion of virtue-signaling. It's this thing of being committed when we want to, and an attitude where we sacrifice in small ways, to make ourselves feel a little better. It's like, *at least I'm doing my part!*

Let me ask you this. If you belong to this religion, if you are so good, then why do you need God? A better question for virtuous living people: If you get your satisfaction from loving yourself, and from your feelings, then why do you waste your time dipping in and out of church? Why pray or read the Bible? Because following Jesus isn't necessarily about a feeling, it's about integrity and truth. No, I'm not starting a new religion called Virtuous Living. But I sure as you-know-what know a lot of people posing as Christians who are actually all about serving themselves. Here are the beatitudes:

> *"Blessed are those who are persecuted for righteousness' sake, for theirs is the kingdom of heaven.*
> *"Blessed are you when others revile you and persecute you and utter all kinds of evil against you falsely on my account. **Rejoice and be glad**, for your reward is great in heaven, for so they persecuted the prophets who were before you."*
> *-Matthew 5:10-12*

Jesus says, *"This is definitely what is going to happen to you as a Christian."* Persecution. Whoa. Whoa. Whoa. For me that's not *"woe, woe, woe... is me,"* it's whoa — hold up! As in time-out, wait a minute. That's not what's going on down the street at other churches. Whoa.

84

That's not what is being advertised on church websites and social media! Time-out. It's not the Christianity advertised all over America today that we are singing about in our little concerts. My friend, you cannot worship yourself to righteous living. You cannot attend church enough times to gain salvation. *Wait Pastor...isn't this is a religion that gives me what I want, now, and if I don't have it, then it means I ain't doing it right? Just teach me how to do it right.* You have it all wrong. You have it all wrong.

This is the last Beatitude Jesus gives on the side of that mountain. Notice that the first and the last have the same statement, *"for theirs is the kingdom."* These Beatitudes have been probing you, and you didn't know it. You think that you have been on a journey for God? It's the other way around. These poetic, gut-checking statements by Jesus have been searching your soul. Jesus has put them in order. There's no way you can start at this Beatitude before all the others. It can't be done. Before you mistakenly start here, go back to chapter one. Jesus reminds His disciples,

> *"If the world hates you, know that it has hated me before it hated you. If you were of the world, the world would love you as its own; but because you are not of the world, but I chose you out of the world, therefore the world hates you."*
>
> *-John 15:18,19*

Christians are persecuted all over for the sake of righteousness because of their loyalty to Christ. Real loyalty to Jesus is like sandpaper to the world. It rubs them the wrong way. Mention Jesus in public and everything goes quiet, or people are ready to pounce. There is major persecution going on in this world that most of us just aren't aware of. Notice it's not *'Blessed are the persecuted,'* but *"Blessed are the persecuted for righteousness' sake."*

Do you know anyone who has been persecuted for Christ? Anyone who has ever been beaten or tortured for their stand for Christ? Please don't think it's just something that happened in centuries past. Several years ago, we traveled to the northeast section of China. My son, a friend, and I were within five miles of the North Korean border. Two weeks before we arrived, our host had made plans for us to meet with a local pastor who was bold for Christ. He was Chinese but was sneaking into North Korea and sharing the Gospel and giving out Bibles. Also, several North Koreans were sneaking over into China to be discipled by this pastor. It was a clandestine effort that resulted in many coming to Christ and wonderful things done in the name of Jesus in that region. But one day this pastor was deceptively lured out of his house by North Korean communist soldiers posing as seekers who wanted Bibles. He went out to meet them, and never came back. They embedded an ax in his skull. We got there just days later, and the church members were devastated. We prayed with them. My friend paid for the funeral and gave money to the pastor's wife. And in this intimidating world, the Gospel goes on. And the words of our Lord to us are, *"Blessed are those persecuted for righteousness' sake, for theirs is the kingdom...."*

I remember when I was at the University of South Carolina in the Eighties there was a student Christian group on campus that preached at lunchtime every day on the pedestrian bridge, the Pickens Street Bridge. The student-preachers would climb up on a bench in middle of the walkway to be seen and heard. As students walking by heard them, they rebelled in a verbal assault. They abused and threatened the street preachers. Those student-preachers were courageous and genuine in their bold and continued proclamation of the truth. I had nowhere near that kind of confidence to stand up for Jesus forty years ago! It was hard preaching, and it was a difficult calling, but this Beatitude doesn't say, *blessed are those who are persecuted for being a fanatic for God.* Fanaticism may lead to persecution, but fanaticism is never commended in the Bible. Having difficulty with being a Christian in your boldness isn't what He is talking about here. There are two kinds of martyrs: the ones who take pride in being talked about for being a Christian, and the ones who live in complete obedience to Christ knowing the circumstances can kill them.

86

Some have mixed politics with Jesus. Yes, you should stand up for what you believe and your political principles, but don't confuse this Beatitude with you being called out for your political stance. If you want to suffer politically, go ahead, but don't blame Jesus if this Beatitude is not verified in your life. This is not a one-liner to soothe your general suffering. So, what does this Beatitude mean? Simple — it means to live a righteous life. Living right?! Who would want to persecute someone who lives right? I agree, it doesn't make any sense. Can someone who is sincerely following the Lord Jesus be abused, you ask. And at this point, you may do some self-examination and discover, *I'm not being persecuted.* Then the following question is for you: *Are you really following Him or are just into virtuous living?*

Why are the righteous persecuted? Good, noble, climate activists are rarely persecuted. Nice protesters for the woke culture are seldom mistreated. Most of the world wants to be decent and we discover that, if we put our minds to it, we can all make some good choices, good decisions, and good sacrifices. All of us are bound to stumble upon a good thing to benefit mankind every now and then. When we make those good choices, it's like patting ourselves on the back — *Hey self, I'm proud of you! You did good.* But the righteous in Christ are persecuted for something entirely different. The Pharisees, those religious leaders of the first century, hated our Lord. They despised Him. Wait, He healed scores (probably many more). He fed the hungry. He visited the lonely. He loved the unlovable. He forgave the unforgivable. So why did they hate Him? Because He was different.

There was something about Him and the way He moved, the way He spoke, and the way He preached, that condemned them. Look at the modern-day evangelistic church: When a disaster occurs and godly men and women are suddenly on sight to lend aid and help clean up, all is well. But let that same group stand up against abortion in today's progressive society, and they are scorned. The Pharisees felt all their right living was made to look showy and cheap by the Lord, and they were right. They hated Him for that. The righteous in Christ don't have to say anything at all. The lost feel unhappy and condemned just because of who they are. The prophet Daniel was hated, and it wasn't because of sweeping reforms he made, it wasn't because of having eight homes, three vacations spots, and fifteen cars. They hated him because of who he was — a man who stood on the principle that God is always right — and his determination to live righteously.

> *Daniel, brimming with spirit and intelligence, so completely outclassed the other vice-regents and governors that the king decided to put him in charge of the whole kingdom.*
>
> *The vice-regents and governors got together to find some old scandal or skeleton in Daniel's life that they could use against him, but they couldn't dig up anything. He was totally exemplary and trustworthy. They could find no evidence of negligence or misconduct. So they finally gave up and said, "We're never going to find anything against this Daniel unless we can scheme up something religious.*   -Daniel 6:3-5

Do you think that making up stuff about a political candidate is a twenty-first century tactic? Long before Russian collusions, Chinese spies, and rogue FBI officials were deceiving people, there were enemies of God. And in the New Testament, they hated the Lord Jesus. This first part of this Beatitude in Matthew 5:10 tells us three things:

#1 Many have the Wrong Impression

If our impression of the Lord Jesus Christ is one where non-Christians applaud or admire Him, then we have the wrong view of Him. The effect of Jesus was that people threw rocks at Him. Big rocks. Rocks as weapons of destruction. The religious right even wanted to harm Him. Why? They hated Him. They detested Him so much that instead of putting a cold-blooded murderer to death, they chose Jesus as the substitute. Isn't it incredible that Jesus died in our stead, that He was our substitute on the Old Rugged Cross, and to get there He had to be a substitute for a vile criminal? People today say they admire Jesus, but if they had seen Him, they would have picked up rocks, too. They hated Him.

#2 It Tests our Impression of Him

What is your definition of a Christian? If you asked most on the street this question, their likely response is, *they are meek, kind, quiet, easy to get along with, and they won't blame you, and they don't offend others, oh yeah, they love.* Look at how Jesus defines a Christian:

> *"Woe to you, when all people speak well of you,*
> *for so their fathers did to the false prophets."*
> *-Luke 6:26*

The influential Welsh protestant minister Martyn Lloyd-Jones once said, "The real Christian is a man who is not praised by everyone."

#3 It makes a Lasting Impression

To become a Christian there must be new birth. There is no other way. There must be a fresh start in your life. We must get rid of the old nature, or the natural man/woman, and cling to the supernatural person in Christ. If you imitate Jesus, this world will love you, but if you become Christlike, it will hate you. He is not of this world. Our salvation is alien to this earthly life.

On another trip to China about six years ago, my friend Don Kenney and I, along with our children, were invited to an underground church meeting. *Underground* means it's illegal. The pastor, Pastor Han, was gracious and kind to us. Talking through an interpreter we learned of his boldness and bravery for the Gospel. He had been threatened repeatedly. Many are thrown into prison for the Gospel in China. The government infiltrates local bodies to spy on congregations, and they single out certain leaders to be persecuted, or even murdered. We heard through sources about three years ago, that Pastor Han was killed. *"Blessed are those persecuted for righteousness sake, for theirs is the kingdom...."*

Do you really know what it is to suffer for the sake of the Gospel? If I were you today, I would re-think my position about the white-collar Jesus we often pursue, this bless-me Jesus we crave, this make-me-feel-good-about-myself Jesus we have been falsely led to serve. Ask yourself — *Do I know the truth of the Gospel? Do I know the true Christ? Have I been fooled?* If you believe Him and understand the Gospel, then Paul's words to the church at Philippi should not alarm you.

> *For it has been granted to you that for the sake of Christ you should not only believe in him but also suffer for his sake.*   *-Philippians 1:29*

No one likes suffering. If you could pick your suffering, then it wouldn't be suffering. It is the essence of suffering that we despise. Am I suggesting to you that you need to go out and look for a fight? No. Should I go and sell everything I have and follow Jesus? That's not a bad idea. I've read where our Lord mentioned that to someone somewhere. But what I am telling you today is to get serious about Jesus. I am urging you to know that life hangs by a thread and eternity is real. And just because you don't feel it today doesn't mean His message isn't real. Realize, then, that we are not here just to grab our slice of spirituality. We must be obedient to Him even if it leads to ridicule or sorrow.

You see, all these Beatitudes outline the definition of a Christian. After spending so much time in them myself, if someone came to me right now and said, "Help me to grow as a Christian," I would say to spend about a year in the Beatitudes before you start anything else. And so, before we conclude this book on the Beatitudes, let me show you at least three principles that emerge from this preamble to the Sermon on the Mount:

A Christian Is Wholly unlike a non-Christian

Why is he different? Because Jesus is different.

> *"Do not think that I have come to bring peace to the earth. I have not come to bring peace, but a sword. For I have come to set a man against his father, and a daughter against her mother, and a daughter-in-law against her mother-in-law. And a person's enemies will be those of his own household. Whoever loves father or mother more than me is not worthy of me, and whoever loves son or daughter more than me is not worthy of me. And whoever does not take his cross and follow me is not worthy of me. Whoever finds his life will lose it, and whoever loses his life for my sake will find it."* —Matthew 10:34-39

The Christian is not just like everyone else, only with a slightly different mindset. He is entirely different. We, who are in Christ, have a different nature altogether.

A Christian's life is structured & dominated by Jesus

> *"Blessed are you when others revile you and persecute you and utter all kinds of evil against you falsely on my account."* —Matthew 5:11

Why are they (we) persecuted? Because we are living for Jesus' sake. In this one verse we can deduce that our whole goal in this Christian life is to live for His sake, to live for His glory. If you know you have been bought with a price, the price of the blood of Jesus, then you will want to live for Him. You desire to present to Him your all, your soul, your mind, your body, and your heart. This one thing differentiates us from everyone else who is not a Christ follower: we want Him to govern our lives. If we are truly Christ-followers, then we will desire, no matter if we slip and fall, no matter if we fail in practice, to glory in His name and to live to bring Him honor. Our goal every day is to live for Christ.

A Christian's life is dominated by thoughts of Heaven

"Rejoice and be glad, for your reward is great in heaven, for so they persecuted the prophets who were before you."   *-Matthew 5:12*

This world today does everything it can not to think about the world beyond. It's almost like a conspiracy in the present, to avoid thinking about death. I understand that to think about heaven means to stop thinking about making more money, to stop seeking the pleasure of this life, to give up the so-called entertaining, fun life. I get it, but I also understand it is why we are different. We know all those other things don't really bring us lasting joy. They are temporal. They are rusting and decaying. Jesus says, "Rejoice! Our reward is yet to come!"

Our culture loves halls of fame. We have a hall of fame for everything. My friend Dave Greenbaum grew up in Canton, Ohio, the home of the Pro Football Hall of Fame. When you don't live there, the Hall of Fame has a certain mystique, and there is a certain draw for football fans to visit the shrine. Dave said after growing up there and passing by the Hall of Fame building every day, it becomes no big deal. It's the same with heaven for some. They have grown so used to the talk of heaven that they don't see it as a big deal anymore. But have you ever thought of heaven and how lavish and extravagant it must be? I find that even those words are poorly chosen to describe it!

The difference between the Christ follower and someone who is lost in their sin is this: Sinners want to be in any hall of fame, and the Christian wants to be in the hall of faith. Hebrews 11 is the Hall of Faith and, just like every hall of fame, has an induction ceremony and, like every induction ceremony, it shows the highlights of their career. It's a fascinating, faith building, God-honoring and glorifying chapter.

> *For he was looking forward to the city that has foundations, whose designer and builder is God.* -Hebrews 11:10

> *For people who speak thus make it clear that they are seeking a homeland. If they had been thinking of that land from which they had gone out. they would have had opportunity to return. But as it is, they desire a better country, that is. a heavenly one. Therefore God is not ashamed to be called their God, for he has prepared for them a city.* -Hebrews 11:14-16

> *He considered the reproach of Christ greater wealth than the treasures of Egypt. for he was looking to the reward.* -Hebrews 11:26

> *Others suffered mocking and flogging, and even chains and imprisonment. They were stoned, they were sawn in two. they were killed with the sword. They went about in skins of sheep and goats. destitute, afflicted, mistreated—of whom the world was not worthy—wandering about in deserts and mountains, and in dens and caves of the earth.*
> *And all these, though commended through their faith, did not receive what was promised, since God had provided something better for us....* -Hebrews 11:36-39

What is the reward? The Bible does not tell us much about it, and for good reason. This finite mind can't grasp such a level of glory or light. We can't define it, nor can we picture it in our heads. Hollywood can't recreate it on our flatscreens. What do we mean we can't define it? Take *love* for example. It's a great word, it's a great thing. But we have so degraded it that we attach it to everything, until it doesn't mean love anymore. Take the word *awesome*. If everything is awesome, then what's truly awesome?

Let me tell you what is lovely and awesome. The Bible says we shall see Him, as He really is. We will see His glorious presence. Our bodies will be changed, glorified. No disease, no sickness, and no pain. There will be no sorrow, no sighing, and no tears. No war, no rumor of war, no separation, no sadness. There will be nothing to make us unhappy even for one second. Purity and wonder — why shouldn't we think about that? It's why the Christian sees the death symbol of the Cross as something glorious. Because it points us to Him and His glory. How often do you think of heaven? The secret of all those people in the hall of faith is that they thought about heaven. They didn't hone in on their suffering and persecution for being a Christ-follower. They looked far beyond that. And if you are being persecuted today, your response isn't one of retaliation, or revenge or even bad talk. It's, *they don't understand...and even those in the hall of faith that the Bible talks about, before me, were persecuted in the same way.* Pray for those who put you down and make fun of you. You were once like them, and God was patient with you. The Apostle Paul said, *"For to me to live is Christ, and to die is gain."* This is what it means: there is something far greater than this. Think about heaven. Blessed are those persecuted for righteousness' sake, for theirs is the kingdom of God.

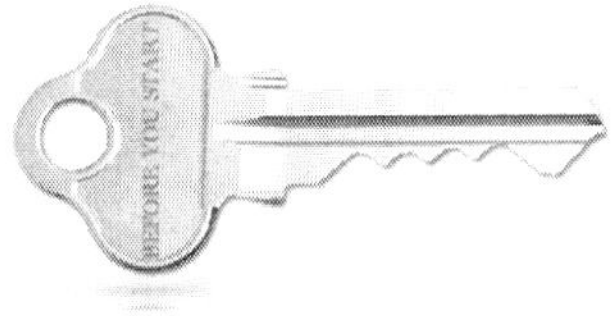

Attitude #9 • Moving Day

"You are the salt of the earth, but if salt has lost its taste, how shall its saltiness be restored? It is no longer good for anything except to be thrown out and trampled under people's feet.

"You are the light of the world. A city set on a hill cannot be hidden. Nor do people light a lamp and put it under a basket, but on a stand, and it gives light to all in the house. In the same way, let your light shine before others, so that they may see your good works and give glory to your Father who is in heaven."   -Matthew 5:13-16

I fear much for many professing Christians. I see no sign of fighting in them, much less of victory. They never strike one stroke on the side of Christ. They are at peace with His enemies. They have no quarrel with sin. I warn you, this is not Christianity. This is not the way to heaven.

-Bishop JC Ryle

Today is your moving day. The move is from the attitude of the Christian to the action of the Christian. I find the Sermon on the Mount remarkable. These aren't jumbled up words, nor is Jesus' sermon boring or difficult to follow. Jesus isn't into amusing the crowd. The Sermon is not filled with a bunch of funny stories and a poem at the end because the preacher has run out of stuff to say. Jesus is not wearing skinny jeans. He's simply outlining the Christ-filled life.

It begs the questions: What have we been doing? Why has the church fallen on difficult times? It's because we have not read, studied, and heeded the words of our Lord and King. Here it is, black and white. Plain and simple. The Beatitudes — it's who you are supposed to be in Christ. So, what do I do? Pack your bags and leave the reign of sin behind and go on with God.

Jesus had seen the crowds. He walked up onto the mountain, and He opened His mouth and started speaking to the hearts of the multitude. It is here that we realize the two main functions of the Christ-follower:

- The Christian is the **SALT** of the earth
- The Christian is the **LIGHT** of the world

Often, I hear conversation where people who have been through difficult times, maybe even a near death experience, respond, "Well, God must have left me here for something, and I'm still trying to find out what that is." Look no further! It's staring you right in the face in this Beatitude. Your job as a believer and Christ-follower is to be salt and light. Quit buying into that talking game of bewilderment as if you are expecting to find out God's purpose like finding buried treasure. This is it! Salt and light. If you think God is holding back on you as a Christian about His goal and function for your life, then you don't understand the Scriptures. It's plain. Salt and light. If you avoid this or gaze beyond it, then you are not telling yourself the truth. This is Jesus saying to you loudly, *"I know what I want you to do! Be SALT and be LIGHT!"* Let's look at them one at a time:

SALT

You are the salt of the earth. What does this imply? Simply, it means that the world is rotten. It has become polluted and gives off a foul odor. The world stinks! It's what the Bible says. God does not like

96

the smell in His nostrils. We live in a fallen world. Its tendency is evil and war, in people and in nations. Left to itself it festers and spiritual disease occurs. It's happening right now. The Bible is full of endless illustrations on this. God made the world perfect, but when sin came in, we see the rotting begin. Just get to the sixth chapter of Genesis and you find God regretting the creation of man. And that is only six chapters in!

> Then the Lord said, "My Spirit shall not abide in man forever, for he is flesh."   -Genesis 6:3

Whatever this means, we do know one thing: it means God is separating from us. Are these the saddest verses so far in the Bible? Maybe so. Subsequently God sends the flood, but it was the principle, it was the heart that God illustrates to us through this calamity. Because just a short time — maybe a hundred years, maybe a thousand — and then there is the nasty grotesqueness of Sodom and Gomorrah. Man's heart got so bad and went so rogue that it was an immoral free for all. Adultery, homosexuality, and plain debauchery described the twin cities. Lot, Abraham's nephew had taken his family and gone to live in Sodom, but as things escalated and chaos ensued, God rescued Lot. He told him to get out and don't look back, but as they got out of town, Lot's wife looked back and Scripture tells us she turned into a pillar of salt. So, what are the implications of salt?

#1 Salt Implies a DIFFERENCE

Christians are different. Salt is a savory spice we add to our daily food intake for the purpose of realizing a better taste. The Christian is essentially different from everybody else. He or she is as different as the salt is to meat when it is rubbed in. As different as the salt is from the wound into which it is poured. The external difference still needs to be emphasized and stressed in our world today. We are true difference-makers. Our goal is to make a difference in the life of people for eternity. Salt does that.

#2 Salt Implies PRESERVATION

Isn't it obvious in this messed up progressive woke culture? We need to be the salt of the earth to preserve our children, to preserve marriages, to preserve our communities, to preserve our families, our nation, and the church. *Preservation means to keep from damage and harm.* This world specializes in damaging and harming all God institutions and His decrees. Parents, please read this carefully: Your main job is preservation — not isolation, not imitation nor intimidation, not probation, not admiration — but an admonition of the Lord Jesus to your children, leading to salvation in Him.

#3 Salt Implies FLAVOR

Without the Holy Spirit walking and moving on this planet, life is boring. Look at the proof by looking at the people who have pursued pleasure after pleasure, good time after good time, substance after substance, until everything is tasteless. For the hedonist, life loses its flavor and becomes savorless. Many get to the end of their lives and still must drug themselves in various ways because they still feel the need of a savior. Our job is to salt the world. Bring real flavor.

My grandmother loved salt and loved to cook with it. She was appalled at salt-substitute. In today's health-conscious world, there are numerous studies on the dangers of salt, but on her table, there was always a big saltshaker. She cooked religiously with it. On a large scale today, the church has substituted the real life in Christ for one that has no flavor, no purpose or meaning.

Here's the test: When you walk into a party, does the conversation change? On the golf course, do your buddies watch their language around you? At church, do people gravitate towards you? Are your words and actions encouraging, or discouraging? Do people respect you, or have regard for you? Do others see Christ in you, even if Christ is not in them? If you can answer yes to these questions, then you are probably acting as salt. You are controlling the tendency of verbal and physical pollution and putrefaction in day-to-day activity, then you are spreading light. If not, then you have lost your flavor, and the lights are out. Jesus says at this point you are no good but to be thrown out, and you are being walked on.

Remember, Jesus starts *the Sermon* by talking about who you are. Let's stop for a moment and look at a social America. The present situation of the world calls for a comment on what it means to be salt. Jesus is certainly not commanding us to make salty pronouncements on the world, to Wall Street and the district. He is not telling us to impose religious principles to Washington and the political establishment. That would be a terrible misunderstanding of *the Sermon* and this Scripture. Never does Paul comment on the policy-making of the Roman government. The church that gets off on the side streets of politics, and onto the roads of social restructuring, will lose its way.

Historically, our nation has survived numerous times the assault of hell by the church reviving and understanding it is salt. The trouble with the church today is that it has far too few people acting as salt. Far too few! We've substituted the taste of God in this world with the search for a feeling. I would put it this way: the church is serving up microwaved religion. Market-minded ecclesiastical groups have packaged a convenient Jesus.

What is the answer? The church must pray, then pray more. If the gospels point to the event of Jesus clearing the temple of moneychangers a couple of times, proclaiming our Lord's words, *"It is written, 'My house shall be called a house of prayer,' but you make it a den of robbers,"* then, we must move more and more towards being a praying body again. I see it over and over in the life of my own church. God moves in answer to our prayer. If we are going to be salt and light, we must go to Him every morning. What are you praying for? Do you keep a prayer journal, where you write your prayers down? You need to at least keep a running list in your Bible to remind you to pray.

Tasting and seeing His goodness means to go to Him in prayer. Your job is to share the Gospel of Jesus Christ in your community and to preach the Word of God through living it out by example, if not also in word. As a pastor, I know that if I spend most of my time talking about how my church can protest, demonstrate, and boycott against social change, and wokeism, then when am I going to teach and preach the Gospel? I'm not saying there is never a time to confront the enemy with a righteous indignation and rebellion, but as Christians we are known as salt and light first. I have experienced first-hand numerous times where, if we as a church get lost in our mission, others are waiting to take advantage of us financially or socially. We have a job, and job number one is to be concerned about sin, to preach the holiness of our great majestic God, pointing people to Christ, so that we see them changed one by one. Salt makes a difference, salt preserves, and salt adds flavor to this dull, stale, tasteless world.

LIGHT

There is the correct assumption of darkness to be considered. When Jesus says, "*You are the light of the world*," we are reminded of what a remarkable and glorious thing it is to be a Christian. Consequently, you and I are responsible for light in darkness. Yet the world has always talked over darkness by disguising it with neutral pastels. Three hundred years ago it was the Enlightenment, or the Age of Reason, that dominated the philosophical world in the late seventeenth and early eighteenth centuries. Intellectualism and cultural movements began to take precedence over faith in God. Two hundred years before that, it was the Renaissance during which there was a political and cultural push tied together. It introduced the idea of humanism which ultimately led to socialism and communism. And even before both of those world crusades, it was the Greeks who

100

stressed their philosophies of life with the likes of Socrates, Plato, and Aristotle. They all came spouting their wisdom of the world before the time of Jesus. Going back to the Enlightenment, it marks the beginning of the wisdom movement in America and it is still going on today. The Enlightenment was the beginning of the attack on the authority of the Bible. And, really, this is the root of all our problems as Christians in the modern era.

Notice that the world has advanced tremendously in knowledge of the mechanical, the scientific; in communication, travel and, of course, technology; and in power, with weapons of mass destruction. But when it comes to the existence of man, when it comes to the knowledge of what to do with all this information, and when it comes to knowing the Truth, we are still in dreadful darkness. We have multiplied our institutions and organizations repeatedly yet, clearly, they have nothing to say. What peace treaty has brought lasting peace? What philosopher has figured out life? What entrepreneur has created the righteous way? What government has figured out social bliss? What progressive measure do we take next to insure another six thousand years? Jesus knows and He says, "*You are the light of the world.*"

One of the greatest themes of the New Testament is that it's not the philosophers or the supreme minds on the planet, but ordinary people, who have been given the wisdom. The Apostle Paul says,

> *For since, in the **wisdom** of God, the world did not know God through **wisdom**, it pleased God through the folly of what we preach to save those who believe.*   -1 Corinthians 1:21

And it's the one thing that appears to be utterly ridiculous to the world — the pure wisdom of God. Jesus says, He is the light of the world. Scripture says, *God is light and in Him is no darkness at all.* So the result of it is, Jesus tells us, *you and I* are now the light of the world. Simply put, the Godhead, or the Trinity — the Father, the Son, the Holy Spirit — has taken up abode in your life.

I call this chapter Moving Day because we've got to move on with the business of being light. And it's easy to determine if someone truly is a Christ follower. If you are, then you are giving light. If you are, then you are growing in Christ and are producing spiritual fruit. Warning, here's the reason so many are having a difficult time these days in truly believing, in true faith in Christ: we don't understand that living in truth and wisdom means we will always be in the minority. The skeptic and unbeliever says, *listen, if this were true then everyone would believe.* That's not what God says. The wisdom of God is foolish to the rest of the world. It doesn't make sense.

So, what does being light in this world mean?

Light EXPOSES darkness

What is the purpose of darkness? It hides stuff. It hides our sin. Why don't people turn to God? Because they are mortified and are hiding from God. Go back to the Garden of Eden scene in Genesis 3, and we see that God came looking for Adam. Where was Adam? He and Eve were hiding. Hiding from what? Whom? From God. Sin makes us ashamed. We are pronounced guilty, and we know it. And if we don't know the way out, if we can't see because of the darkness, what do we do? We keep groping around, falling, and bumping into walls. We will do what we have always done or what has been done before hoping for a different result. Maybe we get smart about money or strike it rich, but after a while, when the luster wears off, we are back to where we started — in darkness. Here's what has happened:

> *...the light has come into the world, and people loved the darkness rather than the light because their works were evil. For everyone who does wicked things hates the light and does not come to the light, lest his works should be exposed. But whoever does what is true comes to the light, so that it may be clearly seen that his works have been carried out in God.   -John 3:19-21*

Light EXPLAINS darkness

What is the problem in the world? It's that we are estranged from God. The light of the world exposes the world, and this bad news. Yet we have been made by God, so the only way to truly live is in a right relationship with God. A great way to put it is that we were made by and for God. Every problem in this world, personally and corporately and internationally, is the result of sin, selfishness, and self-seeking. Sin explains it, and you will not recognize it apart from the light of the world — Jesus. And here's the thing you must comprehend, apart from Christ: we absolutely love sin. We can't get enough of it. We love it and we live for it. In reality, it owns us. The problem we have is not our intellect. It's our nature. It's the human heart because it's always been a heart issue. If you are struggling in trying to decipher the correct answer for living, remember it's your heart (that old nature) that will keep you from going on with God. Maybe the problem is tastelessness of today's Christian. Maybe you've heard enough, and witnessed enough, from saltless Christians who have attempted to cover their light under a basket. And if that is the case, please see now that you desperately need to bow completely to Him and His reign in your life. This world is dark and tasteless. The daily news tells us the blind continue to lead the blind. If you are in a pit with no ladder, up the creek with no paddle, then hear the Gospel. It is all about the Good News of Jesus coming to your rescue.

Did you grasp Jesus' words? Salt that has lost its taste is no good. It has one function. Light covered up is useless. It has one function. In other words, the person who is trying to imitate Jesus is useless. It's the person who is in Christ; it's the Holy Spirit in them. There are many who claim to be Christians, but the Lord said they are far, far away from God. Don't be deceived. Light shines the way to and for God, not on our selfish selves. The Apostle Paul warns Timothy,

> *But understand this, that in the last days there will come times of difficulty. For people will be lovers of self, lovers of money, proud, arrogant,*

abusive, disobedient to their parents, ungrateful, unholy, heartless, unappeasable, slanderous, without self-control, brutal, not loving good, treacherous, reckless, swollen with conceit, lovers of pleasure rather than lovers of God, having the appearance of godliness, but denying its power. Avoid such people -2 Timothy 3:1-5

Light shows us how to ESCAPE darkness

Light exposes and explains darkness, but the good news is that light also shows the escape from darkness. We've tried to escape on our own, haven't we? We've tried knowledge. We've tried education. We've tried politics and being involved in political action. We've tried the conferences, the movements, and the social action. We've tried the self-help stuff, we've tried sports, entertainment, money — we've tried and tried. But the self is fallen, it's polluted and living in a polluted world. Is there hope? Oh yes! There is abundant and everlasting hope. Jesus says, *"You must be born again."*

What you need is not more light, you need a new nature. That is, a heart that will love the light and hate the darkness. It's the exact opposite of what most people do these days. You need someone to take hold of your life and I promise, Jesus will not let go.

Before you begin every day, maybe before you end every day, go back to the Beatitudes. It is an outline for daily Christian living. It's humility in its core, and it is submission to Him at the least. As a Christian, understand these are dark days. God has called you to be salt and light. We are living in a world with neighborhoods of men and women caught up in gross, foul darkness. They will never have light, never experience the flavor of Christ in their lives, unless you are their salt.

Before you decide to quit remember, our Lord saw us as sheep without a shepherd. He had great sorrow in His heart for His chosen people. He was not concerned about Himself. He had compassion for the multitudes. And that is how we are to live in this world today. Did you ever notice in Scripture that after Jesus healed someone, the people gave glory to God and they said, *we've never seen anything like this before.* The light had come. We are to live our lives before others so that we become a conundrum for them. Let them scratch their heads and say, *we can't figure them out!* Let our actions and reactions to life cause them to question us, *why are you so different?* We are to become reflectors of our King. He is light in us, we are to be light to the world.

Acknowledgments

My wife, Missie, keeps me on the path by challenging me and championing me daily as a pastor and leader. Her faith and stamina as a helpmate astound me. She is the encouragement God designed and gave me to preach, lead, and walk with Christ.

This is my fifth book and my assistant, Karen Hulvey, has been my editor-in-chief the whole way. Her ability to design and format the copy is fantastic. Thank God for Karen.

Fresh Church is a beautiful and sweet fellowship of believers where God made me shepherd. We are growing in faith in the Lord Jesus every day. Every person is important to our mission in our community. They pray for me, and they encourage me as they follow. Soli Deo Gloria!

About the Author

Dr. Greg (GD) Dowey is the Founding Pastor of FRESH Church in Chapin, South Carolina. Pastor Greg is devoted to building a great church to the glory of God —Soli Deo Gloria. He is passionate about expository preaching, short-term missionary work, and writing for the purpose of discipleship in the local church. Pastor Greg also enjoys an occasional round of golf and running several times a week.

Pastor Greg holds a Doctor of Ministry from North Greenville University, a Master of Divinity from Southwestern Baptist Theological Seminary, and an undergraduate degree from the University of South Carolina. He and Missie, his wife of thirty-one years, are founders of Simple Ministries, a mission to supply Bibles and preach the Gospel around the globe. They have one son, Jack, a schoolteacher in Birmingham, Alabama.

Other Books by GD Dowey

Eight: The Book About Just One Chapter
ISBN 978-1-7359876-0-6

A study of Romans 8, perhaps the greatest chapter in the Bible. Dr. Dowey reminds us of the freedom we have in Jesus Christ and shows us that walking with Jesus is a new beginning and that God is more interested in our transformation as believers than the political and geographical alteration of nations.

The Great Go Mission
ISBN 978-1-7359876-1-3

In this book, Dr. GD Dowey gives deep personal insight into short-term mission projects and challenges the reader to GO, whether it's across the street or across the globe. He lays a Biblically-based and historical foundation, then follows the changes in missions—both good and bad—and offers recommendations for how to get started and how to GO.

Joy123

ISBN 978-1-7359876-2-0

Jesus won when He died for us and pointed the way to joy for us. In JOY•123, a concentrated study in the book of Philippians, Dr. Dowey reveals Paul's joy in Jesus Christ— In spite of his circumstances— and how others can apply its precepts to achieve this joy in their lives, too. And when you realize joy in Christ in your own life, you are FREE!

1...2...34 Get Your Faith Up Off the Floor
ISBN 978-1-7359876-3-7

A fresh look at Psalm 34 from the ground up.

If your heart is broken, you'll find God right there; If you're kicked in the gut, He'll help you catch your breath.
— Psalm 34:18 MSG

Dr. GD Dowey, in his 4th book, takes an in-depth look at Psalm 34. The Psalms, more than any other book in the Bible, has changed his life. It can change yours, too.

All books are available in paperback from major online book retailers. Some titles also available in Kindle e-book editions from Amazon.com.

112

Made in the USA
Columbia, SC
29 August 2024